EXOTIC WEAPONS OF THE NINJA

EXOTIC WEAPONS OF THE NINJA

SID CAMPBELL

A Citadel Press Book
Published by Carol Publishing Group

To my loving daughter Kim

First Carol Publishing Group edition—1999

A Citadel Press Book
Published by Carol Publishing Group
Citadel Press is a registered trademark of Carol Communications, Inc.

Editorial, sales and distribution, and rights and permissions inquiries should be addressed to Carol Publishing Group, 120 Enterprise Avenue, Secaucus, N.J. 07094.

In Canada: Canadian Manda Group, One Atlantic Avenue, Suite 105, Toronto, Ontario M6K 3E7

Carol Publishing Group books may be purchased in bulk at special discounts for sales promotion, fund-raising, or educational purposes. Special editions can be created to specifications. For details, contact Special Sales Department, Carol Publishing Group, 120 Enterprise Avenue, Secaucus, N.J. 07094.

Manufactured in the United States of America

10 9 8 7 6 5 4 3 2 1

Library of Congress Cataloging-in-Publication Data

Campbell, Sid.
    Exotic weapons of the Ninja / Sid Campbell.
      p. cm.
    Originally published: Boulder, Colo. : Paladin Press, ©1994.
    ISBN 0–8065–2063–9 (pb)
    1. Ninjutsu weapons.   I. Title.
U167.5.H3C357   1999
355.5'48—dc21   98–52804
                                          CIP

CONTENTS

ACKNOWLEDGMENTS

I would like to thank Jon Ford, Editorial Director of Paladin Press, for his artful expertise during every stage of this comprehensive work. Without his guidance and creative input, this work would not have been shared by millions of martial artists worldwide.

I would like to also thank Nancy Lee, Ed Evans, and Gordon Lyda for their many days of photographing the ninja operatives in action. Much appreciation is in order for my friends at Swan Photo Express.

A special heartfelt appreciation for my many students and friends who contributed to this work. Among them are Donna Lyda, Gordon Lyda, my brother Eddie Campbell, Darryl Inouye, Dennis Dickerson, Larry Mah, Nick Palma, Jay Fetters, Dennis Ingram, Nathan Humperies, Jason Humperies, Joe Oliverez, Crystal Swan, Davis Quan, Harold Sinclair, Ed Evans, and Warren Nelson. Great memories that will always be remembered.

PREFACE

Exotic Weapons of the Ninja was written for the serious martial artist who wants to delve beyond the mere superficial in learning about and understanding the weapon crafts developed and used by the infamous ninja warriors of feudal-age Japan. It is a subject that includes virtually every type of weapon art imaginable!

The ninja were among the most clever and insidious super spies the world has ever known. If the ingenious and deadly weapons invented by these *ninpo* assassins are any indication of their cunning and skill, this book will undoubtedly give you a true perspective of their impressive talents.

The weapons and weapon arts described in this book only reflect the traditional or orthodox arts employed by the ninja of ancient Japan. Because there were so many variations and improvised weapons actually used by the clans that inhabited the remote rural areas of Japan, it would be impossible to include everyone in a book of this size. However, the majority of the weapons and weapon systems included herein should suffice in giving you a true representation of the many types of unique weapon-tools at the ninjas' disposal.

While compiling a weapon-oriented book of this nature, two critical factors were always at the forefront of my mind. First, present the subject in a factual manner so that the read er can grasp the essence of the subject matter. Second, attempt to clearly explain the topics in such a way that the reader can assimilate how these ancient ninja weapon arts were actually used in combat. The latter is definitely more difficult to convey than the former. I have tried to present both as best as I could without elaborating too long on only the traditional topics usually associated with weapon-oriented books. I hope this attempt will not only give you a deeper understanding of the subject but further enrich your knowledge of how these rare and seemingly forgotten weapons were really used during Japan's past.

GLOSSARY

Ashiko–spiked foot bands
Bakuhatsugama–short-handled kusarigama with a container of explosives, poison, or blinding powder
Batto-jutsu–defensive swordsmanship
Bo–staff
Bo-ryaku–strategy
Bojutsu–staff fighting art
Chigi-riki–ninja mace
Cho-ho–espionage
Chunin–ninja clan subleader
Fukedake–blowgun
Fuki-ya–darts
Fundojutsu–chain fighting
Goton-po–five elements of escape
Hachimaki–sweatband
Han bo–3-foot staff
Hanbojutsu–halstaff fighting
Henso-jutsu–disguise and impersonation arts
Hishi-bishi–natural caltrops
Hojojutsu–tying arts
Hojutsu–shooting arts
Iaido–sword-drawing art
Inton-jutsu–escape and concealment

Jojutsu–stick fighting
Jonin–ninja clan leader
Jukenjutsu–bayonet
Jutai-jutsu–grappling
Jutte-jutsu–truncheon/iron fan
Kagi-nawa–grappling hook
Kagi–hook
Kakute–iron rings with protruding spikes
Kakure-jutsu–stealth
Kama, Gama–sickle
Kamayari–sickle spear
Kasha–pulley
Katana–samurai sword
Katon–using fire
Kayaku-jutsu–fire and explosive arts
Kenjutsu–offensive swordsmanship
Kinton–using metal objects for distraction
Kiri–single-pointed pick
Koppojutsu–striking arts
Kuda bashigo–tube ladder
Kunai–digging and leverage tool
Kunoichi–female ninja
Kusarifundo–weighted chain
Kusarigama–weighted chain and sickle
Kusarigama-jutsu–chain and sickle arts
Kusari–chain
Kyojitsu tenkan ho–philosophy giving more meaning to
  survival and accomplishment than to engaging an enemy
Kyomon–practical education
Mamukigama–kusarigama with a poisonous snake
Manrikikusari–10,000 power chain
Metsubishi–sight removers
Metsubushi–art of invisibility
Mikkyo–secret knowledge
Musubi bashigo–single-cable loop ladder
Naginata–halberd

Naginata-jutsu–halberd fighting
Nawa–rope
Neko-te–"cat claws"
Ninja-ken–ninja sword
Nitoryu–two-sword style
Noroshi–using signal fires
Oh-gama–battlefield version of the kusarigama
Rokushaku bo–6-foot staff
Ryu–school
Sageo–scabbard cord sash
Saya–scabbard
Seishin teki kyoyo–spiritual refinement
Shikomi-zue–hollowed-out staff and canes
Shikoro–saw
Shinobi-iri–stealth and entering techniques
Shinobi-shobo–short shank of rounded wood or iron
Shinobi-shuko–assassin spiked hand bands
Shinobi-zue–ninja staff and canes
Shinobigatana–ninja sword
Shuko–spiked hand bands
Shuriken–throwing star
Sui-ren–water training
Suiei-jutsu–swimming and fighting in water
Suiton–using water
Sumo–grappling
Tai-jutsu–unarmed combat
Taihenjutsu–silent movement when stalking a prey or escaping
Taka bashigo–high ladder
Tanegashima–firearms
Tanto-jutsu–knife fighting
Tekken–ornamental band slipped over the foreknuckles
Tetsubishi–steel foot spikes
Tobi bashigo–leaping ladder
Tonki, Toniki–personal arsenal
Toritejutsu–arresting technique
Tsuba–sword handguard

Tsubo giri–boring tools
Tsubute–stone-club throwing missile
Tsuri bashigo–hanging ladder
Yamabushi–warrior mountain priest
Yari-jutsu–spear fighting
Yari–spear
Yugei–traditional education

INTRODUCTION

"There he is!" shouted the leader as the trio of sword-wielding samurai vassals gazed upward into the darkened ceiling vaults. "Behind the beams near the ledge! Just be careful, these *shinobi* dogs can be pretty dangerous when they're cornered!"

"Move the lantern higher so I can get a good look at him!" came another order from the leader. "Keep your *katana* drawn and ready!"

The ninja assassin remained calm while contemplating his fate, satisfied with the knowledge that he had successfully stolen Lord Toranaga's valuable war plans and had them safely tucked away in his *obi*. Now the question he asked himself was, "How do I get out of this unexpected situation?" Though he had been in similar circumstances many times before, this was the first time that his *chunin* (ninja subleader) had given him erroneous information about the structure of a castle interior. "Was it a double-cross or unintentional?" he questioned while his mind raced to figure out his plan of escape.

A quick account of the events that had occurred during the past several hours flashed through his mind as he applied pressure to the deep sword slash on his upper forearm. Getting into the heavily guarded fortress, climbing through the murky, stench-filled secret passageways leading to the chart and map room, eliminating two samurai sentries, expending his supply of *tetsubishi* (steel foot spikes) to delay three pursuers in the narrow stone corridors, breaking the blade of his *shinobigatana* (ninja sword) while prying open a locked transom above the stable quarters, exhausting his supply of *shuriken* (throwing stars) while outmaneuvering a dozen staff guards near the watchtower, and using his complete supply of *metsubushi* (sight removers) in order to make good his escape through the shogun's private living quarters. If it had not been for the *shuko* (spiked hand bands), *ashiko* (spiked foot bands), and his reliable *kagi-nawa* (grappling hook), it would not have been possible to reach this lofty sanctuary high in the beams now overlooking his newest adversaries. His mind returned to the painful state of reality as the final knot was tied on the makeshift bandage he had improvised from a *hachimaki* (sweatband).

Getting through the bastion window on the adjacent wall 15 feet away was going to be another formidable challenge with no equipment remaining except his *kama* (short-handled sickle), the only remaining *shuko*, a 12-foot section of *kusari* (chain) which was still wrapped around his waist, and the last *tsubute* (stone-club throwing missile). He peered from the darkness, trying to remain invisible to the three samurai warriors below. Vacillating between the impending dilemma and the many experiences of his past, the ninja operative wasted little time in choosing a *shinobi-iri* (stealth and entering technique) that would serve both his escape and defensive purposes.

As the samurai vassals sought diligently for a means to apprehend the intruder from the darkened vault chamber and oak beam abutments, the ingenious shadow warrior swiftly and cleverly set his own multipurpose plan into motion. With an eerie silence, he unwrapped the *kusari* from his waist. As each loop was meticulously unfurled from his torso, he coiled it around the open palm and shoulder of his wounded left arm. After this necessary task was completed, he reached deep into his utility pouch and withdrew the last of his weapon-tools. Fumbling with the loose *sageo* (scabbard cord sash), he used the razor-sharp sickle blade and cut off several short sections, one of which he fastidiously attached to the handle end of the *kama*. Moments later, after tying the cord to one end of the *kusari* and looping the remaining section of *sageo* through the hole in the stone *tsubute*, a makeshift *kusarigama* (weighted chain and sickle) was improvised. It was a last desperate effort to complete his dangerous and important mission successfully.

During this crucial process, while narrowly avoiding detection by his anxious captors, the *shinobi* carefully moved behind the turreted ledge parallel to the massive wood beams. Even as the three warriors continued to gaze upward into the shadows, they were beginning to doubt their own previous observations. The flicker from the hand-held oil lantern, combined with the shadows cast by the overzealous searchers against the damp stone walls as they moved about randomly, cast uncertainty into their minds as to the actual presence of the intruder.

"Quiet," grunted the leader. "Don't move! Let him make a move so we can be sure where he is. Takahashi-san, get a spear from the armory!"

Suddenly, before his order could be carried out, a blur of motion emanated from the shadowy depths high above their heads. A fierce arcing slash severed the arteries on the side of the leader's neck. An instant later, another accurate lightning-fast snap induced a similar mortal wound on his compatriot. The weight of the spinning chain combined with the hatchet-like blade was sufficient to incapacitate even the most noble of warriors. The lantern bearer, before he knew what had happened, was suddenly ablaze as the fragile lamp virtually exploded before his eyes as it was struck by the tremendous force of the chain and handle section of the *kusarigama*.

With two mortally wounded warriors spurting blood from the large veins in their necks and another staggering in hysterical confusion, the fleet-footed ninja operative leaped across the lower beams onto the ledge leading to the transit 12 feet below the turret vestibule. Without stopping to calculate his actions, he hurled the bladed end of the *kusarigama* skyward. The moans of agony nor the flaming figure storming through the cold castle corridor had little effect on him as he skillfully tossed the hooked blade of the weapon-tool through the rectangular stone window opening.

With a smooth, careful pull to ensure that the makeshift single-pronged grapple hook had set, the ninja began ascending the damp stone wall. Seconds later he "vanished" through the tiny opening and down the outside of Toranaga's castle fortress, leaving behind a trail of death and discord among its inhabitants, none knowing who he was or what he wanted!

• • • • •

This brief account of the feudal-age ninja warrior's clandestine affairs was intended to acquaint you, the reader, with how important weapons and weapon-tools were to these warriors of darkness. This book was written exclusively to reveal the awesome arsenal that the *ninpo* agents had at their disposal. By thoroughly absorbing the information found herein, you will discover why the ninja of yore were such feared and dreaded stealth operatives.

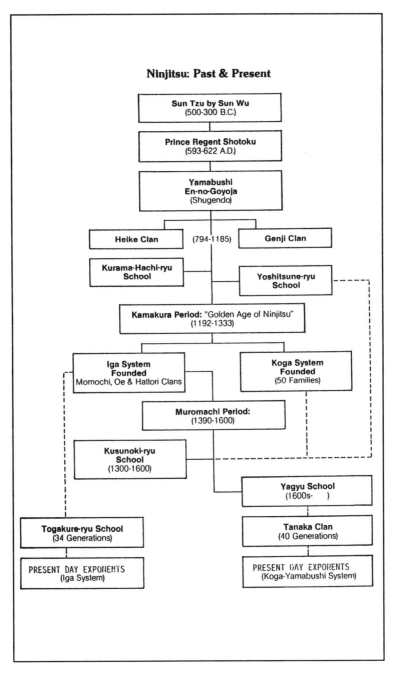

Ninjitsu: Past & Present

Sun Tzu by Sun Wu
(500-300 B.C.)

Prince Regent Shotoku
(593-622 A.D.)

**Yamabushi
En-no-Goyoja**
(Shugendo)

Heike Clan   (794-1185)   **Genji Clan**

**Kurama-Hachi-ryu
School**

**Yoshitsune-ryu
School**

Kamakura Period: "Golden Age of Ninjitsu"
(1192-1333)

**Iga System
Founded**
Momochi, Oe & Hattori Clans

**Koga System
Founded**
(50 Families)

Muromachi Period:
(1390-1600)

**Kusunoki-ryu
School**
(1300-1600)

Yagyu School
(1600s-)

Togakure-ryu School
(34 Generations)

Tanaka Clan
(40 Generations)

PRESENT DAY EXPONENTS
(Iga System)

PRESENT DAY EXPONENTS
(Koga-Yamabushi System)

Chapter One

SICKLE WEAPONRY

In actuality, the *kama* (sickle), or *gama*, has been in use for centuries in most Asian countries, mostly by peasants in the fields to harvest rice and other staple grains essential to their survival. Depending on the length of these hand-held cutting blades, the *kama* could be used in a number of ways. The shorter, wooden-handle versions could be used for digging and scraping, as a *kiri* (single-pointed pick, also known as *tsubo giri*), as a fixed-blade knife for whittling and shaving, or merely as an all-purpose bladed instrument used in the preparation of foodstuffs.

Since the peasants of feudal-age oriental countries were not permitted to own or possess weapons because of their inferior caste status, any form of military armament such as swords, spears, and shields was totally prohibited. However, bladed weapons such as scythes, fishing gaffs, and short-handled spades, as well as staffs used to carry parcels, goods, or water, were necessary to perform daily routine agricultural and fishing tasks. Therefore, when used for those purposes, the tools aroused very little suspicion and posed no threat to the ruling authorities who imposed these restrictions on their subjects.

Because of its bladed configuration, the *kama* earned the reputation among the peasants as being a primary agricultural tool that could also serve as a clever, yet discrete, makeshift

The ninja warriors were masters of contriving clever ways to convert common harvesting implements such as a sickle into deadly weapons.

Oriental hand-held sickles came in a variety of shapes and forms. The shinobi assassins of feudal Japan could use them all with equal proficiency.

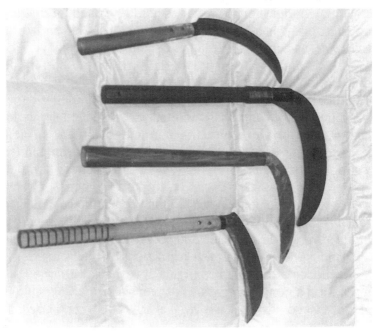

A unique technique used by the shadow warrior was to connect two sickles at the butt ends of the handles with a sturdy section of iron chain. When this improvised weapon was mastered, it posed a more lethal double threat to unsuspecting adversaries.

weapon when they needed to defend themselves against aggression. The feudal-age ninja operatives, many of whom were of the common caste, saw the martial advantages of this farming implement early on, and it soon became a vital part of their secret weapon-tool arsenal.

For close-range combat, the short-handle versions could be used for cutting, slashing, gouging, severing, ripping, and stabbing, much as with any form of hand-held knife or bladed weapon. Because the razor-sharp blade was mounted at a perpendicular angle to the end of the handle, many oblique and unusual angles of attack could be executed. Also, as with most hooked or 90-degree-angled weapon-tools, penetrating stab and slash techniques could be performed. The handle gave the tool weight and distance, therefore permitting a greater amount of devastation without putting the user in

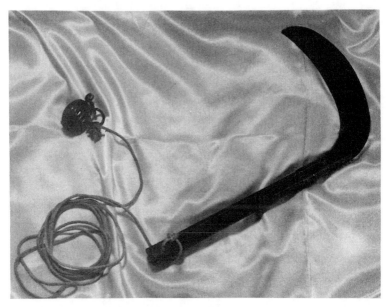

Another common modification to the short-handled sickle was to connect to the butt end a section of cord with a hefty weight. This offered the ninja a broader range of protection.

jeopardy against an opponent with an inferior-range weapon.

Defensively, the hooked blade had unique uses that could not be performed with a straight-bladed, short-handled weapon. The adjoining blade/handle connection could be used for blocking, snaring, locking, diverting, intercepting, restricting, deflecting, and trapping techniques. But the ninja were also highly cognizant of the drawbacks of shorter-range weapons such as the *kama*, especially against longer traditional weapons employed by their arch rivals, the noble samurai vassals of the era. The sturdy, exceptionally sharp samurai weapons such as the *katana* (samurai sword), elaborately designed *yari* (spear), *kamayari* (sickle spear), *naginata* (halberd), bow and arrow, and later on the *tanegashima* (matchlock pistol and rifle, introduced by the Portuguese in 1542 A.D.) posed serious threats to even the most skilled *kama* wielder.

To attempt to equal those odds, the ninja relied upon their deviously ingenious imaginations. It is historically uncertain whether these clandestine operatives actually invented this type of weapon-tool, since longer-handle scythes were also employed to cut and harvest sugar cane and other forms of stalked produce. It is, however, generally recognized that the ninja modified the existing versions to give them greater range. This evolutionary process is thought to have begun by their attaching cord, and later chain, to the handle end of the shorter versions of the *kama*. Naturally, chain was much more effective and less likely to be severed by sharp-bladed weapons, although cord attachments or braided horse hair or hemp fiber did have advantages when silence was required.

When the short-handled versions of the *kusarigama* (weighted chain and sickle) were introduced for strictly combative purposes, an object was affixed to the opposite end of the chain or cord connector to balance and counter the

Ninja agents who had already mastered the use of sickle weaponry trained less experienced members of the clan. This training usually began at the age of 5 and lasted well into their adult years. The traditional method of learning began with observation.

weight of the sickle. Not only did this increase the control of the weapon-tool, but it automatically introduced many other weapon uses that could not be performed otherwise.

To appreciate the ingenuity of the fabled ninja stealth agents of ancient Japan, each section of the *kusarigama*—the sickle, chain or cord connector, and attached counter-weight—must be considered as a weapon-tool in its own right. The chain or cord connector had obvious uses as a weapon-tool for strangulation, whip maneuvers (much like a modern bullwhip), tripping, lassoing, restraining, and fouling an opponent's weapon attacks. When doubled several times, it could be used as a sort of chain mace or flexible truncheon, cat-o'-nine tails, or any other form of weapon where varied length and flexibility were required to serve offensive or defensive needs.

The stone or metal weight, before being attached to the connector, had been used for hunting and combative purposes since the dawn of civilization. When carrying out their clandestine missions, the deceptive ninja clan members always kept these seemingly primitive uses in mind when all other means of weapon combat had been exhausted.

When used as a single, complete weapon, the *kusarigama* was a complex and devastatingly lethal weapon-tool that required much practice and refinement if it was to be utilized effectively. Complicated technical manipulations took the form of spinning twirls, convoluted unfurling methodology, quick ambidextrous retrieval techniques, and double-ended cutting and striking movements. The skilled user also had to learn how to avoid being struck by his own spinning weapon; synchronize body and weapon movements into one smooth offensive or defensive strategy; foul an enemy's attack while counterattacking with the other end of the weapon; modify the length of cord or chain while swiftly changing distances against the adversary; coordinate the timing with spinning, rolling, and ducking while dealing with several armed opponents at the same time; accurately throw the *kama* so that the blade and point struck first; execute intricate strangulation

The deadly, razor-sharp blades of the sickle played a vital role in silencing samurai sentries . . . generally on a permanant basis!

techniques while retaining control of each end of the weapon; and all of the other stealth, climbing, and grappling techniques generally associated with only a weighted chain.

For the ninja who had undertaken the awesome task of truly mastering the *kusarigama*, this meant quite a few years of dedicated daily training. The *chunin* (subleader of a ninja clan) and, in rare instances, the *jonin* (clan leader) would never permit an operative to use this versatile weapon-tool in the course of an assignment unless he was confident in his agent's skills. Since it was such a versatile weapon-tool, if an agent mastered these arts, it generally meant that he could minimize the amount of weapon-tools needed to carry out an assignment. For that reason, the *kusarigama* was deemed an essential implement, and rigorous training in its use was started at a very early age.

After the short-handled *kusarigama* techniques were mastered, the ninja began training on the longer-handled versions. Because of the larger, heavier wooden staff sections, the balance and timing were drastically altered. Adjusting to the tech-

The sickle blade could also be used to cut or hack open wooden dowel locking pins that separated ninja operatives from their objectives.

niques using the *oh-gama* (battlefield version) took a tremendous amount of tenacity and determination. Because of the enormous size and weight of this weapon, it could easily entangle the legs of and trip warhorses. Once the samurai warrior was thrown from his steed, the large axelike blade was used for slashing, thrusting, and ramming the felled enemy. These techniques, again, took many years of training to master.

During a young ninja's tenure while learning this unique weapon-tool, he was gradually introduced to the more stealth-oriented techniques. Some of these ruses entailed learning to use variations of the basic *kusarigama*. One in particular was known as the *mamukigama*. This innovation was just like the standard *kusarigama* except that a poisonous snake was tied to a section of the chain or cord near the weighted chain end. As the ninja swung and twirled the connector at the enemy, he attempted to entwine it around the opponent's torso or neck. Once the serpent came in contact with him, the results were inevitable.

Another variation was known as the *bakuhatsugama*. The

only difference between it and the short-handled *kusarigama* was the fact that a fragile container of explosives, poison liquids, or blinding powders was affixed to the weighted end. Again, the results were obvious when it struck the enemy!

As with all weapon-tools in the ninja operative's vast arsenal, the *kusarigama* gave him extraordinary abilities once he had mastered its peculiarities. The *kusarigama* was indeed a lethal and devastating weapon when put in the hands of a warrior who concerned himself with carrying out his assigned mission rather than saving his own life. It was a weapon that he could use to take his own life just as easily as that of his adversary—vengeance in the truest sense of the word!

Chapter Two

STAFF AND CANE WEAPONRY

Prior to the discoveries of metals such as copper, bronze, and iron, crude weapons of the staff genre sufficed in serving man's needs in times of war. Whether they were sharpened at the ends or had various shapes and configurations of hand-chipped stone appendages, these prehistoric staves, pikes, and spears were generally considered to be the primary weapons used by ancient civilizations around the world. The ninja of feudal Japan were among the first to exploit the entire spectrum of military and utilitarian uses for such simple and mundane weapon-tools. Their art evolved from the acquired knowledge amassed over centuries. The *ninpo* warrior commonly referred to the art as *bojutsu* (bo = staff + jutsu = art).

As a makeshift weapon-tool originating from the stone age, the *bo* (staff) had undergone many subtle changes by the time it had arrived in the golden age of *ninjutsu*. However, it was not until that time that the ninja clans inhabiting many areas of rural Japan began to really utilize the common staff to its fullest martial extent. Among some of the innovations contrived by these wizards of deception were clever adaptations of staffs, which were hollowed out and chain or cord weapons secretly concealed inside; poisoned liquids or powdered eye irritants deployed with ingenious plunger systems; variations in blowgun weaponry with sophisticated sighting methods;

fixed and articulated flexible attachments with spiked or bladed weighted metal objects attached to the other end; and even ornate symbolic religious adornments affixed to one or both ends which, in addition to being deceiving, could very easily be converted

The longer version bo was the most common of stick weapons. The entire art of bojutsu was formulated around the rokushaku (6-foot staff).

to lethal weapons themselves.

From the purely tactical perspective, the ninja categorized their staff tools into three distinct classifications. However, exceptions were made when personal preferences or a fixed or articulated addition was included to radically convert a *bo* into an altogether different type of weapon. This was the case in situations when the desperate ninja agent had to create another type of tool using the basic walking stick or staff to ensure the successful completion of a mission.

The three categories of *bo* were primarily determined by

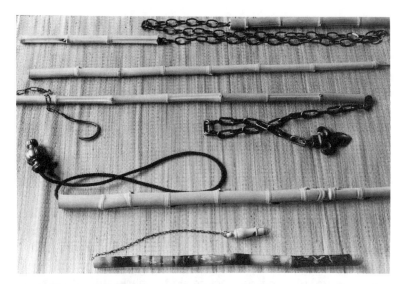

Hooks, chains, weighted metal truncheons, gaffs, and bladed weaponry were among the insidious objects that could be concealed within a ninja staff or cane. Even flutes (bottom) could be converted to improvised garrotes to silence an adversary.

The enemy was in for a rude awakening if he confronted a ninja operative wielding a concealed dagger inside his staff.

Another secret weapon that could be concealed inside a hollow staff was a stilettolike spear. These simple weapons could be designed so that a flick of the wrist could force the spear to shoot out of the tube.

the range for which each was best suited. Ultimately, a range (distance from an adversary) was predetermined to compensate for the distance between a ninja and an opponent wielding a weapon that had lesser or greater range. Essentially, the longer-range staff weapons varied between 6 and 12 feet, the mid-ranged ones were between 3 and 5 feet or so, and the ultra close-range staffs were from several inches beyond the width of the hand to a little over 2 1/2 feet or so in overall length. This established a basic foundation for the many diverse and unique *bojutsu* fighting arts that each ninja operative was trained in throughout his or her life.

The greater-ranged staff weapon-tools were used most effectively against adversaries wielding traditional-length samurai swords, spears, halberds, or staffs of a similar reach.

The mid-ranged *bo* was most effective at closer distances where actual physical contact could be made with an enemy. Many of the techniques used at this distance required the use of leverage, pressure point attacks, arm locks, joint techniques, and restraining tactics. Also, in certain situations the *ninpo* operative could use medium-range staffs in much the same way that he could use the longer ones. Of course, this normally meant modifying body and feet maneuvers to compensate for the distance that the staff itself lacked in reach.

A makeshift blowgun could be assembled using a hollow cane and poisonous darts. The blowgun was ready for use when a false bamboo plug was removed from each end.

An innocent-looking walking cane could be converted into a plunger-actuated water gun that could spew eye irritants at an unsuspecting enemy.

Another uncommon use of staff and cane weapon-tools was as underwater breathing tubes when such tactics were needed to fulfill a mission.

The ultra close-range staff weapon-tools were often cleverly concealed within the *shinobi's* garments and brought into play after some elusive or surprise tactic had been implemented. The hand-held, clublike staffs were ideally suited for close-range techniques involving strangulation; gouging strikes to the vital organs; attacks to the eye, nose, and ear cavities; securing wrist locks and arm-bars; and reinforcing fist or open-hand punching, striking, or blocking techniques.

It is uncertain whether range determined the actual offensive and defensive techniques or if it was the required self-defense tactics themselves that ultimately were responsible for determining which type of techniques would be applied in a given combat situation. Does the weapon determine the technique, or does the range determine the type of weapon employed?

The *ninpo* warrior's shrewd, analytical mind dwelled extensively on this subject when it came to actually anticipating or engaging in mortal combat with a samurai vassal. The resultant tactical wisdom revealed that three different yet highly related qualities had to be artfully incorporated with any of the staff weapons if total effectiveness in actual combat was to be achieved. Training, distance (from the opponent), and leverage formed the perimeters for *bojutsu*.

Training, the first of these essential staff-fighting prerequisites, became a specialized affair after a type of staff weapon-tool was selected for a particular ninja operative or when structuring a strategy against a certain type of weapon. Range, being the second necessary quality, was directly affected by the length of staff wielded compared to whatever the enemy was using. Rather than elaborate on hypothetical nuances, the ninja began at an early age learning the importance of spatial mobility. Knowing their own speed and how quickly they could get from one point to another; mastering many types of footwork; learning to read fake and unintentional movements from an enemy; coordinating weapon maneuvers with spins, twirls, swinging, or reaping techniques; developing a keen sense of reflexive responsiveness when blocking and countering an opponent's aggression; intercepting and redirecting an oncoming attack while focusing on the counterattack coup de grace; using deceptive fakes and creating intentional openings in their own defense in hopes of drawing the enemy in; and incorporating extension sliding techniques that gave the staff fighter a greater range without forewarning the enemy were all vital regimens of training that each ninja had to undertake with any of the *bojutsu* weapons.

Next came an extensive phase of training with each staff weapon in the refined art of using leverage both passively and aggressively. Regardless of whether the stick was a short hand-held truncheon or a long quarterstaff, each type had certain specialized leverage techniques uniquely suited for it. A ninja staff expert realized that the longer staff weapons had enough weight, length, and heft to partially create its own leverage once the stick was in motion and crashed into an enemy or his weapon. He was also cognizant of such elements of time, distance of travel, amount of physical force put into a technique, anticipated intentions of an armed adversary, angle of impact needed to cause the most damage to the enemy or his weapon, and the expected effects of the amount of accelerated leverage applied when the force of the impact reached its target.

On the other hand, the *shinobi* was knowledgeable in the causes and effects of leverage in the sense generally associated with the laws of physics. He practiced techniques in which all or a portion of the longer or shorter staffs could be maneuvered through, around, over, under, or between an enemy and/or his weapon to force him to submit, remain restrained, or lose his weapon. The ninja warrior could also cause excruciating pain by forcefully levering the bone structure against the musculature, and use the enemy's weight and body positioning to actually force him to restrict or limit his own fighting abilities. Naturally, each length and thickness of staff weapon had peculiarities that were directly related to the leverage that could or could not be applied in real combat. The ninja therefore spent years mastering the subtleties of each and every length of staff.

When the proper training, associative distances for a certain length staff, and appropriate leverage techniques were applied with any *bojutsu* weapon, the ninja became a force to be reckoned with even by a warrior expertly skilled in the use of the deadly samurai sword. So potent were his devastating staff-fighting techniques that to become entangled in his elusive web of subterfuge meant certain death, whether it be with a seemingly innocent-looking section of hand-held hardwood shank or a lengthier 10-foot staff. Each in its own right, wielded by a skilled expert in *bojutsu* was capable of producing irreparable devastation!

Chapter Three

POLEARM WEAPONRY

The ninja used the word *hoko* to convey and define the broad range of stafflike weapons in their extensive arsenal. Literally interpreted, *hoko* generally was associated with weapons of the polearm varieties, an array of unique and diverse implements that included the *kama-yari, naginata,* traditional military-issue *yari,* as well as the more obscure types of bladed or spiked appendages that could be readily attached to a staff or pole. Generally speaking, any prefabricated or improvised metal fixture that could be affixed to a stave and used as a weapon could be categorized as a weapon of the *hoko* variety, thus making this *kobudo* classification perhaps one of the broadest categories of collective weapon types within the ninja's entire arsenal. In many cases, because there were so many types of unusual weapons, each almost had to be studied as an individual art until all of its peculiarities and particular offensive/defensive techniques and associated methodologies had been thoroughly mastered.

Whereas many would assume that a pointed, spearlike bladed attachment mounted on a hardwood staff instantly qualified it as a *yari* with very specific fighting functions and purposes, the deceptive *shinobi* operative perceived it from a much broader perspective. Rather than merely being used for poking, thrusting, stabbing, and, in some cases, slashing maneuvers, almost any weapon or weapon-tool within the *hoko* arsenal could be cleverly adapted so that other offensive and defensive techniques could be applied. These techniques included reaping (where the opponent was swept off his feet with the pole section of the weapon), gaffing (where hooked portions of a bladed *hoko* were used to cleat and snare the opponent or his weapon), gouging and digging (when it became necessary to convert it to a common utilitarian implement that readily suited his needs), harvesting (when any of the short- or long-bladed scythes were attached to the staff), chopping (when ax heads were affixed to the staff), throwing (when sharp points were firmly attached to either or both ends), or any other of numerous tactical stratagems, depending upon the shape or design of the attached metal fixture. In essence, the ingenious ninja operatives believed that any staff or pole weapon ultimately should be multifunctional regardless of the type or amount of lethal protrusions affixed to its end.

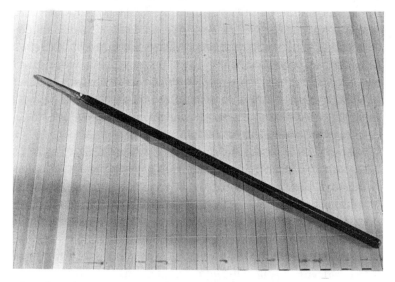

The traditional Japanese yari was only one of the polearm weapons in the ninja's vast hoko arsenal.

With this perspective in mind, the ninja could actually create virtually any type of *hoko* weapon that he might deem befitting for a particular espionage assignment. That is why there were so many rare and unusual polearms within the realm of ninja weaponry. A halberd that had a long, slender, curving blade with a dozen or so barbed spikes attached to the back of it, to the uninitiated, may appear as nothing more than a mere broad ax with some ornate decorative baubles to increase its lethal appearance. Of course, the insidious *shinobi* assassins were not beneath deceiving an enemy in that respect, but the actual functions of the *hoko* were more important than that.

If the ninja operative knew that he was going to be involved in a mission that would require him to engage an armed and armored samurai warrior mounted high atop a fiery steed, then he would want to use a weapon that best suited that particular situation. Obviously, a short-range, lightweight clublike weapon would not suit the purpose. He needed one with a solid, durable handle (to withstand the force of a samurai sword slash), long enough (to remain out of direct range of the mounted enemy), and sharp and weighty enough (to possibly penetrate armor or at least inflict enough damage that the impact alone could temporarily disable the warrior) while still being versatile enough to be manipulated in cramped quarters where dismounted enemies and confused and stampeding horses may be treading.

The curved spikes protruding from the back of a broad halberd blade were ideally suited for hooking, snagging, or gaffing anything they struck on the back swing of an offensive assault or defensive counterassault. A disoriented samurai warrior who had been knocked off his horse could be viciously ripped open with the barbed hooks on the *hoko*. Because of the increased expediency of not having to reposition the heavy halberd to make a second powerful attack, his technique could be executed in a much quicker manner, ultimately killing his foe before he could regain a sturdy upright fighting posture.

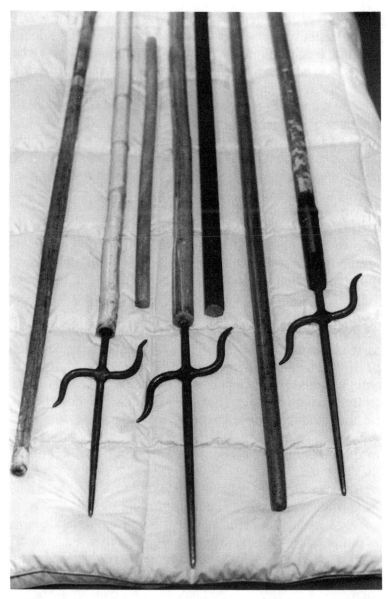

Fishing gaffs, broad axes, canes with hidden bladed tips, and simple pointed sticks were considered part of the the hoko arsenal.

The *hoko* halberd's protruding hooks had other important functions for combat involving foot soldier against mounted warriors. Techniques like using the barbs for severing the rider's reins so that he lost control of his steed or cutting tendons in the horse's legs on a return swing after forcing the rider to lose control were typical examples of how these barbs could be used.

In many cases, the attachments or strange-looking barbs, hooks, blades, or the like on a polearm made it possible for it to be used for purposes other than direct combat. A curved hook mounted to one or both sides of a spike's spear point could very easily have applications that were not necessarily obvious. Either of the prongs could be used for hooking high overhead branches so a ninja could climb to higher elevations. It could just as easily be used for tripping horses or enemies from hidden places along paths, gaffing fish or small game, scaling bastion walls as a grappling hook (*kagi-nawa*), gigging mounted warriors from tree overhangs as they passed

The ninja was not as concerned with military refinement as other warriors in Japan. A simple pointed stick often would suffice.

below, raising or lowering large parcels of equipment that may be needed in the course of a mission, and even snaring a bolted lock by lifting a latch so that it could be opened from the outside. Naturally, these field-expedient uses required the ninja operative to have knowledge of many other aspects of his *shinobi* arts before they were ever attempted with a *hoko* polearm weapon.

Tactically, *hoko* weapons, regardless of the style or configuration, had three distinct characteristics. They provided their wielder with additional range, leverage, and greater power when the appropriate techniques were used.

Range is considered the relative distance of the *hoko* weapon from an armed or unarmed adversary. The ninja were acutely aware that the understanding and practical use of range was almost always a crucial factor in manipulating polearms. In addition to determining when to attack or evade an enemy's assault, the polearm-bearing ninja realized that speed and sharp awareness were also essential. An attack or thwarted movement that was initiated at too great a distance could be countered very easily, while one started in close enough could strike down the enemy before he could react effectively. Also essential was the proper implementation of tactics such as fakes, misdirections, and perception tricks that could get the ninja agent close enough to his adversary to down him. Of course, his expert knowledge and exacting skills in thrusting, reaping, spearing, gaffing, sweeping, slashing, poking, gouging, arcing, throwing, and spinning always contributed to his overall effectiveness while using a *hoko* weapon in actual life-or-death combat.

Another fundamental element in the effective use of *hoko* weaponry was understanding the concepts and repercussions of reach. The ninja realized that reach was not how far he could cut, slash, hit, and so forth with one blow, but rather how far he could effectively perform an offensive or defensive technique without moving his feet a great distance. Correct body movement entailed minimizing stepping and other coordinated body-weapon motions that could actually hinder or diminish the effectiveness of other techniques. Too much movement or overt exaggerations, for example, could forewarn the adversary of the ninja operative's intentions. For that reason, the *shinobi* learned to economize his motion, react swiftly to the opponent's maneuvers, and coordinate his *hoko* polearm fighting technique to coincide with his covert or overt tactical stratagem.

As with the element of leverage, this wisdom usually came into play once actual contact had been made between the ninja, his weapon, and the enemy and his weapon. Simply put, to use a *hoko* weapon properly and fight effectively at extremely close ranges, the *shinobi* had to be extremely adept at maneuvering the polearm while using proper positioning, timing, hand manipulations, foot positioning, and tried-and-true techniques to defeat his adversary without getting cut, maimed, or mortally wounded in the process. The ninja learned to use all of the strongest parts of his *hoko* while keeping the weaker parts out of direct contact with the cutting edges or pointed tips of those of his enemy. Learning to use the *hoko* to keep a safe distance between him and his antagonist made this task a bit easier.

If leverage was properly applied after contact had been made with an enemy and/or his weapon, the ninja could reinforce his position by using fighting principles learned in his armed training. Among these techniques were tripping, trapping, locking, pressure-point attacks, punching, elbow and knee attacks, biting, torquing, joint locks, throwing, sweeping, grappling, side stepping, spitting, raking, ripping the eyes, or simply redirecting the enemy's force of body weight while executing follow-up attacks to vital areas. Naturally, the *hoko* had to be maneuvered in such a manner that the technique complemented the empty hand or weapon ploy if optimum results were expected. To misjudge or underestimate the skill of an armed opponent at the ultra-close ranges where physical contact had been made could be very lethal, especially for one that had become so preoccupied with his own tactics that he chose to disregard the close-range leverage skills of his opposition. Occasionally this happened, and the stealth agent paid for it with his life.

The third crucial element that ultimately affected the ninja's ability to wield and manipulate a *hoko* polearm weapon was actually determined by the inherent characteristics of the weapon-tool itself. This third quality was greater power, referring primarily to the weight, durability of the component parts, and length of the weapon itself. The importance of this may not have seemed so crucial to those who had mastered a single weapon such as a razor-sharp samurai sword, but the ninja had to be concerned with every type of weapon and the advantages and disadvantages each held over others of lesser or greater lengths. Therefore, superiority, range, and leverage perhaps being equal, could usually be determined by the one possessing the weapon with a greater power potential. A weapon that was built shoddily or with inferior parts or materials would certainly be destroyed much more quickly than one of more durable construction. Although the ninja were not as concerned with durability as were their arch rivals, the notorious samurai warriors of feudal Japan, they knew that a weapon had to be strong enough to withstand the force of a sharp-bladed weapon like the *katana*, especially pole axes and battlefield versions of *hoko* that were primarily intended to engage an enemy during formal skirmishes rather than stealth-oriented missions.

By most assessments, the *hoko* weapons were among the most rugged and durable in the ninja operative's arsenal. Virtually every one of their polearms could withstand the most brutal punishment and still remain functional. Many were very heavy (weighing between 15 and 25 pounds), and some of the staff sections could range up to 15 feet in length from the head to the butt end. The really longer varieties of *hoko* had to be manipulated in such a way so as to require the wielder to take spatial availability, lateral movement, distance from an opponent, time to travel to an intended target, and synchronized coordinated harmony of the weapon's movement with the wielder's body positioning into account if it was going to be handled effectively. These longer versions were normally only used by the most skilled ninja warriors, but in their hands they were indeed devastating and highly lethal weapons.

Chapter Four

FIXED AND ARTICULATED STAFF WEAPONRY

Shinobi-zue literally translates to "ninja staff and canes." This arsenal encompassed virtually every stick and staff type of weapon-tool used by the *ninpo* ninja clans that operated throughout Japan in its feudal past. It was an assemblage so enormous and diverse in appearance and application that almost anyone unable to distinguish between them and the utilitarian purposes they also served could easily be misled to believe that they were nothing more than mere walking staffs, *tenbin* poles used for carrying large parcels attached to each end, or canes used by the elderly to steady their steps.

Historically, sticks, staffs, and canes have always served dual purposes in Japanese culture, especially within the realm of pugilism and *ryus* (schools) of traditional weapon warfare. For commoners and samurai caste alike, the necessity to employ simple-appearing bamboo or hardwood staves of varying lengths as makeshift weapons has long been one of the favorite improvised defensive strategies of these two vastly different societies. The staff was, after all, one of the few commonly available weapon-tools mutually accessible to both the peasant class and privileged members of Japanese society.

As weapons, sticks, staffs, and canes were always readily available, unobtrusive, and easily mastered. As with the samurai, who were required to master the staff as one of their

If a staff or cane could be modified to contain a fixed or articulated staff weapon, it was considered to be of the shikomi-zue variety of shinobi-zue weapons. This kept enemies confused—was it a cane or a weapon?

primary weapon arts, the ninja were likewise obliged. Unlike their feudal rivals, however, who received traditional formal training with only a few staffs of standard lengths, the *shinobi* clan members from early childhood were taught many, many more *zue* and *bojutsu*. In many cases, the ninja's staff-fighting arts included training with staffs and canes that were hollowed out (*shikomi-zue*) to conceal blades, chains, hooks, arrows, climbing aids, and even poison liquids and gasses. Some could also be transformed into underwater breathing tubes or silent blowguns, ultimately expanding the practicality of these seemingly simple sticks into something much more lethal and devastating than many of their contemporary staff-trained rivals could ever expect to comprehend.

Next to *seishin teki kyoyo* (spiritual refinement), *tai-jutsu* (unarmed combat), and then *ninja ken* (ninja sword) training, *bojutsu* (stick and staff fighting arts) was considered an essential staple among the 18 levels of training that most ninja agents learned. This reflected its importance as an art deemed necessary to carry out missions of subversion and espionage under oftentimes adverse and potentially dangerous conditions. The art of *bojutsu*, in actuality, was the foundation from which all of the other specialized *shinobi-zue* weapon-tool fighting skills evolved. Regardless of whether a staff or cane had a spiked point, hooking gaff, or flexible chain attached to it, or was filled with poisonous powders, the practical use of the staff section as an implement of self-defense and survival against another armed opponent came first.

There were many reasons for the ninja's approach to learning and mastering the simple staff. First, in virtually every role that they might assume while plying their cunning and stealthy craft, a cane or lengthier staff was a common utilitarian item. This ensured that they were always armed with a tool that could be used to adequately defend against such superior forms of armament as swords, spears, and halberds, these being standard weapons brandished by samurai vassals of that time.

Second, since pointed tips, affixed bladed attachments, or other more lethal extensions increased the range and/or raised the difficulty level of maneuvering a staff properly under crucial combative conditions, it was the ninja's belief that sound, simple, uncomplicated weapon systems and arts could be relied upon with more certainty than those that required years of specialized training. Although most ninja operatives, given years of serious training with a particular

A long rice flail became a lethal articulated staff weapon when used by a skillful ninja operative.

shinobi-zue weapon-tool, were just as adept at it as they were with the staff, the formative years of study with a basic weapon such as the staff made that progressive transition possible. This satisfied the ninja warrior's initial offensive and defensive needs while simultaneously providing the foundation for the more advanced types of *shinobi-zue* weaponry arts. This, all the while, strengthened his appreciation for the basic survival skills against armed enemies.

The third reason for undertaking extensive basic training with the staff was to ensure that all of the known offensive and defensive techniques were learned. As simple as this assessment may seem, there was much more to it than fundamental logic. Most *shinobi-zue* weapons were restrictive in one way or another because of their various lethal appendages. If chains, cords, or other flexible connectors were attached, the advantages that they possessed in one respect could be hinderances in another.

For example, a long chain with a weighted beater at one end became more cumbersome. In most cases involving actual combat against an armed adversary such as a sword-wielding samurai warrior, elements like quick-changing differences in spatial availability; suddenly losing control of the weapon during a crucial moment; adjusting the spinning, looping, and twirling to accommodate a position change of the constantly moving enemy; controlling the staff and unpredictable chain extension after planned or unanticipated contact with an adversary had been made; and modifying offensive or defensive weapon stratagems as the situation warranted were among the basic disadvantages that even the most skilled of specialized *shinobi-zue* ninja could expect under the most ideal of circumstances. Also, because of the inherent design features of each *shinobi-zue* staff or cane weapon, certain restrictions of either lateral, vertical, horizontal, oblique, or twirling techniques could be expected. Most of these complex restricting characteristics never occurred when wielding the common staff.

When the feudal-era ninja became aware that each staff type weapon-tool had its own unique advantages and disadvantages, which usually came as he began serious training with each one, he then appreciated the years spent mastering the fundamental skills stressed while learning *bojutsu*. It was a training regimen as complex in strategic nuances as the stick was in simple appearance. This training began literally from the time that a youth was old enough to hold a stick and comprehend the self-defense purposes of such a mundane object. Around the age of 5 or 6 was common among most of the clans throughout Japan.

Among these first exercises was learning every possible way that the staff could be gripped, developing stances and anatomical movements that corresponded to ideal offensive and defensive methodologies, basic strikes using every part of the weapon, traditional blocking that was commonly practiced in stylized schools of *bojutsu*, improvising on these defensive attitudes while taking multiple opponents and environmental criteria into consideration, participating in mock combat situations supervised by the elders of the family, practicing *kata* (a prearranged sequence of mock self-defense movements where defensive techniques were followed up by offensive counterattacks to various areas of an imagined enemy's body), and then actual controlled freefighting with other equally skilled members of the *shinobi* clan. This in-depth training was undertaken with a wide assortment of typical staff weapons, including the *han bo* (a middle-length staff about 3 feet long), which resembled a common walking cane more than the standard 6-foot versions, up to the staffs that exceeded 11 feet in length.

Because each length of staff possessed inherent self-defense characteristics in accordance with its size, the novice *bojutsu* practitioner then began to train in earnest in the fighting techniques that were best suited for a certain weapon. With the shorter cane-length staves, the mid-range (6-foot) types, and the long ones (9 to 11 feet), one common denominator existed—range or distance. This very important element ultimately dictated the type of real fighting techniques that could be performed with it.

A *shinobi* soon discovered that the *han bo* varieties were best suited for poking, jabbing, single-handed swinging, close-in locking and restraining techniques against the enemy's joints, choking, suppressing an opponent's weapon

A common tenbin could hide a lengthy section of chain. A twist of the staff combined with a powerful spinning manuever instantly converted the staff to an articulated chain weapon.

while getting close enough to execute pressure point attacks, and many other close-range trapping techniques against both the adversary or his weapon. At the medium ranges, which were best suited to the *rokushaku bo* (staffs of about 6 feet in length), more powerfully executed offensive and defensive techniques could be executed. Combination blocks followed by brutal counterattacks to the enemy's vulnerable targets; low-level reaping techniques that could knock the enemy off of his feet; spearing attacks that could be performed with such precision that the end of the staff could be rammed into an enemy's eye socket before he knew the attack had been initiated; and many spinning and twirling assaults were included in these maneuvers, thus, perhaps making it the most suitable range at which staff techniques could be executed without getting too close to an enemy wielding a razor-sharp samurai sword, spear, or halberd.

Though the longer-reaching 9- through 11-foot staffs held advantages in distance from an opponent, unless the ninja operative was exceptionally skilled in the peculiarities of these weapons, they lacked some very important staff-fighting elements. Qualities such as spatial limitations, taking more time to execute a technique because of the greater distances the weapon had to travel before a block or strike reached its target, agile repositioning against an enemy wielding a less cumbersome weapon, and awkward and ill recovery in the event that these offensive/defensive ploys missed their mark were among the typical shortcomings these long-range staffs suffered. Of course, the adept *shinobi* versed in *bojutsu* knew these shortcomings and managed to create ways to avoid them, especially when he had affixed appendages that converted his simple staff into a *shinobi-zue* weapon. A spear, hook, gaff, or the like sturdily mounted on one end had a subtle way of deterring even an armed adversary wielding a shorter-range weapon from foolishly rushing in.

It was only after the three ranges of staff fighting in the traditional sense had been mastered that the ninja operative actually began serious training in the real *shinobi-zue*. With all of the prerequisites and preparatory nurturing behind him, the task of learning how to wield canes and staffs was actually made much easier. Qualities such as timing, agility, dexterity, natural feel for different length staffs, coordinated hand and

With the chain and hook exposed, this monk's staff demonstrates the ninja's insidious ingenuity. Nothing was sacred when it came to improvising deadly disguised weapons.

torso manipulations while remaining stationary or moving, judging distances, spatial and environment considerations, avoidance drills against mock enemies wielding different types of weapons, special tricks, unorthodox fake maneuvers to distract or mislead the enemy, and achieving maximum power and speed from a given technique were covered during this stage of the training.

Under the sagelike wisdom and stern guidance of the clan elders, many of whom were responsible for creating or contributing to the evolution of these unique *shinobi-zue* cane and staff weapons, the ninja began his advanced education in stick fighting. He soon discovered that each and every one of these clever implements had a highly specialized purpose in addition to the obvious ones that were applied in traditional *bojutsu* fashion. For example, when a dried stalk of bamboo had been hollowed out and a spiked blade inserted with a simple trigger mechanism, the innocent-looking staff, with the flick of a finger, was instantly converted into a deadly *yari* (spear), enabling the user the option of using the weapon as a staff until the time was right to unleash his *yari-jutsu* (spear

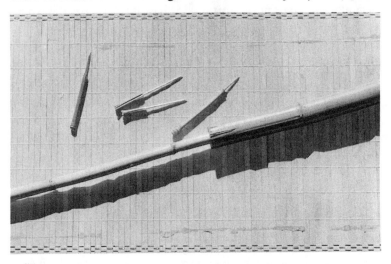

The telescoping sections of the bamboo walking cane reveal a deadly poison dart blowgun.

arts) talents on an enemy. As with all of the *shinobi-zue* weapon-tools, hidden weapons that functioned either separately or in accompaniment with the innocent-appearing staff-cane itself contributed greatly to its overall effectiveness. The element of surprise was the obvious reason for this. Solid extensions such as spiked blades, hooks, gaffs, and the like were generally much easier to maneuver than staffs and canes that concealed flexible appendages such as rope, cord, or chains. With the latter, control, accuracy, proper timing, and calculated interception against an enemy or weapon were the primary elements that became more crucial in a deadly combat encounter. Even with the element of surprise, the articulated varieties—as unobvious as they may have appeared before the concealed attachment was artfully brought into play—required the ninja user to be extremely adept at skills that were not generally of primary concern with the rigid or fixed *shinobi-zue* implements. Among the common advanced obstacles that the wielder had to overcome were complex combination maneuvers where a chain or cord had to be controlled before, during, and after the feed out; tricky lassoing, reaping, swinging, twirling, recoiling, and snap-striking (where the chain or cord section was popped like a bullwhip); retrieving and redirecting a twirling strike; disengaging the weapon from an enemy if the possibility of entanglement was anticipated; mastering long-range garrote techniques; and learning to use both ends of the *shinobi-zue* simultaneously.

This is where the most intense period of mock combat took place with *shinobi-zue* staff and cane weapons. It was also a period when other members of a ninja collective actively tried to deceive and trick the fellow clan member attempting to achieve expert status. They knew, as did he, that every possible deceptive ploy had to be used as a training tool to adequately prepare the shadow warrior for the eventuality that it may be used against him in real combat. With that enlightening perspective in mind, no deceptive ruse or possible enemy weapon fighting technique went unpracticed. This intensive training sometimes consisted of years of tedious practice before the *shinobi* had fully mastered his craft. But it was this preparation and dedication to serious training that made the ninja such feared espionage agents in feudal Japan.

An umbrella could suddenly be converted into a deadly dagger when the handle was removed. This same ruse was used with many other utilitarian tools.

Chapter Five

GRAPNEL WEAPONRY

The innocent-appearing *kagi-nawa* iron grapnel hook with a lengthy section of sisal hemp or braided horsehair rope proved to be more than a mere climbing device when placed in the hands of a skilled and experienced *shinobi* operative. It could just as easily be converted into a lethal weapon possessing awesome destructive power with the same amount of clever ingenuity that the shadow warriors employed when using it for scaling high, fortified castle walls or other seemingly impenetrable barriers that separated him from his tactical objectives.

By definition, the *kagi-nawa* is a basic grappling hook (*kagi*) and a rope (*nawa*) used primarily as a climbing device. In some instances, the larger weighted variations were used as anchors for small boats. However, the *ninjutsu* warriors of ancient Japan were among the first to see the many subversive advantages of such a mundane piece of hardware. When the mountain mystics incorporated the secret art of *hojojutsu* roping techniques, the *kagi-nawa* could almost miraculously be turned into an effective device for snaring, entangling, or binding an enemy. Other more sophisticated and devious methods were employed when the rope was spun and the iron hooks used to claw and rip at an antagonist's vital organs in close-quarter combat.

The *kagi-nawa* underwent some unusual changes and served some unique and unassuming functions for the ninja operative, who relied quite heavily on creative innovation and stealth to complete his or her assigned clandestine missions. Whereas one might logically assume that a grappling hook

The ninja kagi-nawa featured a basic grappling hook and a rope.

was only used for the aforementioned utilitarian functions, the *shinobi* warrior explored every conceivable way that it could be applied as both a tool and a weapon-tool simultaneously. Naturally, his years of training in weaponry and improvisation played a vital role in this assimilation.

Within the realm of these special applications were diverse ways in which virtually every part of the *kagi-nawa* could be wielded artfully. For example, the *nawa* could be readily converted to a *musubi-bashigo* single-cable loop ladder. Stirrups could be formed by doubling the rope and tying overhand knots at incremental distances along the cord. These loops could then be grabbed or used to support the body's weight after the foot had been inserted; the ninja operative could then simply climb up or lower himself. This improvisation made it possible for a *shinobi* warrior to remain suspended for extended periods of time while digging or boring through a bastion wall or other fortification without having to use his hands to support his weight.

Since the ninja were highly adept at creating ingenious devices for breaking and entering into enemy strongholds, all forms of ladders and climbing devices appealed to them.

The grappling hook made it possible for the ninja to reach seemingly impossible heights. Once they had reached one plateau, they would duplicate the hook-and-climb technique until they had reached their ultimate objective.

Though some of these were specifically designed to aid in ascending or descending to higher or lower elevations—including the *taka bashigo* (high ladder), *kuda bashigo* (tube ladder), *tsuri bashigo* (hanging ladder), *kumo bashigo* (cloud ladder), and *tobi bashigo* (leaping ladder)—the *kagi-nawa* rope and metal hardware along with sections of hollowed bamboo rungs and interconnected cords could be easily incorporated to form these versions. Not only were these easy to make for the ninja, but it enabled him to unfold or collapse them swiftly and rather silently and transport them over great distances. The cord of hemp or braided horsehair served many other useful purposes when it was used without the gaff. Simply by removing the gaff, the ninja could modify the *kagi-nawa* to perform such functions as a lasso; pulley rope for traversing ravines or lowering his equipment into deep tunnels too small for both him and his gear to get through together; trip cord for felling enemy-mounted horses; trip wire to warn of impending danger; booby trap to detonate explosive charges; improvised garrote when a stealth operation warranted it; and many other weapon-tool applications that exclusively required the use of a rope.

When the iron grapple was attached, another broad range of unusual improvisations revealed themselves. Such weapon-tool creations could be used to snag a tree branch or open crevice and swing from one place to another to escape from a pursuing enemy. By using several disposable *kagi-nawa*, the ninja could preplan an escape route to traverse ravines, rappel from castle towers, slide down high stone window vestibules, launch himself across vast expanses between treetops, climb laterally across an open space to enter a stronghold or escape from an enemy, and even as a block and tackle when other pulleys were attached. This made it possible for the *shinobi* warrior to raise or lower large amounts of weight (e.g., other equipment needed in a mission), force open locked doors and barred windows, lift trap doors and other weighty obstacles, and the like. These were definitely applications that eluded less knowledgeable individuals.

The ninja's true tactical ingenuity revealed itself when the crafty shadow warrior applied his weapon talents to the *kagi-nawa*. These skills fell into two distinct categories, one being improvised methodology and the other the actual use of the grappling hook as a weapon art in itself.

Improvised methodology was perhaps the most clever of the two since it truly reflected the ninja's creativity at constructing other forms of weaponry from the cord and/or hook sections of the grapple. These derivatives included makeshift staff weapons like the *kamayari* hook spears in which the gaff was affixed to the end of a bamboo or hardwood pole. As a *yari* it was somewhat different than traditional spears employed by the fierce samurai warriors and foot soldiers. Whereas their versions were used for piercing and stabbing

Besides its obvious duties as a grapnel tool, the kagi-nawa could also be utilized as a deadly weapon by the resourceful shinobi assassin.

with the pointed metal blade, the ninja took a more versatile approach. The hook prongs of the grapple could be incorporated into the weapon so that a blend of characteristics were achieved. Some of these qualities were using the curved gaffs to trap, redirect, or suppress an enemy and/or his weapon; gaff in the forward or reverse directions; reach out with the hooks and snag an enemy while the wielder was perched in a tree high above or on some other concealed overhang; and even hook a horse's leg and cause the enemy to topple from his steed. Once this was done, then the makeshift *kamayari* could be used to eliminate his antagonist.

The *kagi-nawa* turned *kamayari* was also ideally suited for other equally important uses. Because it was firmly attached to the staff, it worked extremely well for hooking over a tree branch, castle wall, or ship side, immediately converting it to a climbing tool of another design. Rather than the normally flexible cord associated with the typical *kagi-nawa*, the hardwood staff became the climbing mechanism. The shrewd ninja operative could just as easily apply this climbing technology to such operations as reaching, hooking, and then swinging from one tree to another, from a roof joist to a window ledge, across high ceilings and narrow castle walls, and the like. From the purely utilitarian perspective, the makeshift *kamayari* was just as effective when used as a pole for transporting baggage, supplies, or equipment, or gaffing fish with the inverted prongs.

Since staffs, cords, articulated chains, and weighted metal configurations have always played a vital role in the inventive process these masters of illusion used to create ingenious and insidious weapons, the grapple hook portion of the *kagi-nawa* was obviously well suited to provide the weight for these unique contrivances. Other weapon applications could be found in such implements as the *shikomi-zue* or other sub-class weapons within that category. Hollow bamboo, cord, or flexible chain and various types of hooking or weighted objects formed the foundation for these ninja weapon inventions.

In the case of the makeshift *shikomi-zue*, a hidden chain attached to the gaffing device was stuffed into a hollow staff with only a very small section of the curved prongs protruding. When the time was right and the enemy was within effective range, a cornered ninja operative would unleash his secretly hidden fury. This usually took the form of swinging the well-gripped innocent-appearing staff in a powerful circular motion, all the time calculating the angle and feedout time for the chain and hook to become fully exposed. Within the same motion, the well-timed maneuver was intended to snap outward and hook or circle the enemy's legs, body, or weapon. Once the enemy was ensnared or jerked off his feet, the *shinobi* used the chain, gaff, or staff for necessary follow-up offensive tactics to dispose of his startled adversary. These techniques were usually premeditated and swift!

As a fist-load, close-range, hand-wielded weapon, when the grapple hook was used without the cord or braided rope, it again served some very effective purposes for the ninja who needed to adapt a traditional tool to a warfare situation. As

Grappling techniques often worked best as a team effort. One ninja would remain behind to signal of possible danger while the other scaled a towering enemy wall.

with any hand-held weapon, three or four sharp, pointed, curved protrusions came in handy when skillfully manipulated by a ninjutsu operative well versed in *tai-jutsu* methodology. Any part of the metal section could be used for myriad offensive and defensive applications. Blocking a weapon assault using a predetermined part of the shank or prongs; gaffing an opponent's vital organs; gouging into a restraining hand; piercing the throat with the hooked prongs while simultaneously strangling, ripping, stabbing, poking, and slashing like a knife; and executing *daken-taijutsu* "striking, kicking, and blocking" techniques were also among the common usages when fighting an enemy while wielding the *kagi*. This form of empty-hand combat was even more lethal when the ninja wielded the gaff in one hand and used another weapon such as a *shuriken* in the other.

The second category for using the entire *kagi-nawa*, rope included, was just as unassuming as the first when the techniques were used entirely for combat rather than for its primary purpose of climbing. Again, the ninja's expert use and understanding of the applied applications of roped or articulated chain devices made this method of close-, mid-, and long-range weapon-tool warfare possible. This specialized field of combat included artfully manipulating the rope or cord connector to perform loops, twirls, spins, arcing patterns, subtle or explosive feed-out maneuvers; wrapping lasso techniques; overhead rotations that could be varied with the amount of take-in or feed-out applied; and snap-strike techniques similar to wielding a bullwhip.

The ninja's years of practice and acquired experience in the *kusarigama* (chain and sickle) were especially beneficial when using the *kagi-nawa* in this fashion. By executing the high-speed twirling, looping, and spinning techniques, he could keep a multitude of armed samurai warriors at a safe distance until an opportunity presented itself to make good his escape. Naturally, these evasive ruses were an integral part of the actual fighting techniques themselves, and the ninja used every conceivable means at his disposal to avoid capture by an enemy faction that had discovered his presence during the course of an espionage mission.

These many singular- and multiple-opponent techniques combined with the improvised tactics employed by the shadow warrior while using a seemingly innocent-appearing grappling hook and attached section of rope provide just one example of the many deceptive ways that the *shinobi* eluded and outwitted their rivals. It is also why the *kagi-nawa* was known as the dynamic grappling hook of the feudal-age ninja!

Chapter Six
MACE WEAPONRY

Centuries prior to Japan's feudal past, sticks, staffs, canes, and other wood-handled utilitarian implements were adapted to serve the user's needs in times of combat. But perhaps nowhere in the annals of military history has a sect or clan of people more vividly demonstrated its ability to create lethal weapon-tools from these seemingly innocent items than the ninja of medieval Japan.

There are many unique variations within the ninja's *shinobi-zue* (ninja staffs and canes) weapon arsenal. Some were hollowed out to conceal blades, chains, climbing aids such as rope ladders, hooks, arrows, caltrops, and even gasses, poisonous liquids, and powdered explosives. In addition, once the hidden weapon-tool components had been removed, the long hollow cavity could be converted into underwater breathing tubes or silent blowguns.

The *chigi-riki*, as a weapon within this category, was a weapon-tool that resembled the medieval maces used by Anglo-Saxon warriors and other members of knighthood during the European Middle Ages. Though each style was basically the same in inherent design, there is no documented evidence to suggest that either form of mace was acquired from or inspired by the other. Each seems to have been indigenous to its respective culture before European nations

The ninja chigi-riki was lighter than its European counterpart.

had had direct contact with China or Japan.

By definition, the mace was a clublike weapon of war, often with a flanged or spiked metal head (beater) attached to a rounded section of sturdy hardwood with a length of chain. The European models were heavier and had more heft than their Asian counterparts. Whereas the "morning star," as the Anglo-Saxon versions were known, was developed primarily to penetrate massive armor, chain mail, and jackets of reinforced dry leather, the ninja *chigi-riki* were less obvious in their intended function. This was due primarily to the nature and modus operandi of these clandestine espionage agents. The less that was known about or seen of these shadow warriors, the better it was for them and their anonymous clients. Likewise with the weapons and weapon-tools they used in plying their subversive trade.

Technically, the *chigi-riki* was considered a member of the *furi-zue* family of *shinobi* weapons. Also included in this category was any form of weapon-tool that could be described as having a stick or staff of any length attached to a weighted chain of any length. In the case of the *chigi-riki*, the weighted metal end attached to the chain had sharp protruding spikes fixed in the beater. By description, however, these types of weapons fell under the broader heading of *shinobi-zue* weapon-tools, which included any tubular sections of hardwood or bamboo in which component parts, *metsubushi* (sight removers), or other supplementary weapons such as spikes, for example, could be hidden.

The ninja usually preferred his *chigi-riki* to have an equal proportion of chain to hardwood or dried bamboo. This way he could better control the weighted end and manipulate it accurately when spinning or twirling the weapon. If the proportion varied drastically, it could have encumbered his ability to wield it with authority, even if he was highly skilled in its use. This could have been dangerous to himself to have a spiked metal weight spinning out of control on the opposite end!

Tactically, the *chigi-riki* had many unique qualities. When the chain was concealed inside a hollow bamboo handle, to which it was attached by an iron pin, it could be flung in the direction of an enemy. This surprising feature was often fatal when the spike-laden weight of the beater struck the victim in the head. This characteristic—combined with spinning, twirling, looping an antagonist's weapon, entwining his torso, executing powerful low-level reaping maneuvers to the legs, snapping the deadly spiked weight like a bullwhip, plus using feed-out and retraction methodology for myriad offensive and/or defensive situations—made it an ideal multipurpose weapon.

To better understand the tactical advantages and multipurpose characteristics of the *chigi-riki*, the feudal-age ninja needed to have a broad comprehension of the general principles of the use of articulated weaponry. Only then could the serious art of perfecting and actually applying techniques begin in earnest.

Under the overall heading of flexible weapons, those having jointed connections had more tactical advantages than ones with fixed configurations. Of course, the more complex the articulation arrangement of a flexible weapon, the more adept the wielder had to be to use it effectively.

Because many of the early articulated weapons were believed to have originated from simplified agricultural flails, much of their natural use and physical manipulation were also thought to have evolved from the peasants who became so adept at using them. Likewise with the terminology used to describe many of the component parts and techniques of the *chigi-riki*. The striking weight—regardless of weight, heft, or design—was called a "beater" (swingle or swiple in certain countries). Though the *chigi-riki* was generally considered to be a weapon with a chain as the articulated connector between the beater and the handle, in earlier times (when agricultural tools of this nature were employed as flails), ropes, leather thongs, braided horse hair, or thinner sections of durable cord served a similar purpose.

A peasant with little or no comprehension of tactical weapon warfare undoubtedly had a fairly reasonable understanding of the physical damage that could be inflicted with an articulated implement just through the rote process of using his agricultural tool on a daily basis. Whereas a fixed weapon-tool transferred force down the shaft until it reached its designated point of impact, flexible connectors made it possible to generate four to nine times more impact force with the same amount of exerted energy. In the agricultural sense, this meant that less work could produce a comparable result. The ninja operatives of ancient Japan, like other military factions across the world, recognized the tactical advantages of inflicting more lethal forms of injury on their adversaries with the weapon-tool.

Early in this tool-to-weapon conversion process, the ninja also discovered that the length ratio between the connector, beater, and handle made an enormous amount of difference controlling the weapon. Included in that delicate balance was the inherent weight of the beater and chain, rope, or thong. In designing a specific type of *chigi-riki* or other articulated weapon-tool of the *shinobi-zue* variety, the ninja tried to construct versions where the handle-to-chain length ratio was such that it was physically impossible for the weighted end to strike his hand when the chain was taut. Past experiences taught him that anytime the beater rebounded, either by missing or making contact with a target, it could result in serious injury to the wielding hand(s) or other parts of his own anatomy.

After length-to-weight ratios were comprehended clearly,

The ninja operative underwent an extensive training program with the chigi-riki.

the ninja began focusing attention on the design of the beater itself. Experimentation and foreknowledge of other weapon-tools possessing similar characteristics told them that certain shapes produced different results. Any design featuring spikes or beveled edges concentrated the strike force into a smaller area, thereby inflicting more damage to the recipient. Typical shapes used by many of the ninja clans included square, rectangular, hexagonal, and rounded when pointed spikes were used.

To fully prove the effectiveness of a specific type of *chigi-riki*, the ninja next embarked on an extensive regimen of impact training. Many unique ways of twirling, spinning, manipulating the handstaff, and controlling the length-to-weight ratio were learned.

A form of *chigi-riki* solo training involved striking a wide variety of objects having different densities and firmnesses. Bags filled with dried leaves and wood chips, posts wrapped with padding, suspended straw-filled sacks, and other such targets were contrived for this early phase of training. It was here that the ninja *chigi-riki* user discovered how the flexible weapon behaved in actual use as opposed to swinging, striking, or twirling the weapon in open air. It also showed him what kind of penetration could be expected if and when he encountered an adversary such as a samurai warrior attired in full armor.

One valuable lesson the ninja discovered in solo training was that when a *chigi-riki* weapon struck a hard or bony target, two distinct things could occur. The spiked points of the beater (provided that his weapon had them) could penetrate and remain stuck in the enemy, or the weighted end could rebound violently and temporarily become out of control. This required the ninja to be able to distinguish between the two types and know what split-second course of action to take at the time of impact. To further exemplify the unpredictable behavior of his flexible mace, when the ninja struck soft and yielding targets, the *chigi-riki* stopped dead on impact or rebounded with an unpredictable amount of force. In these situations, he had to learn to automatically anticipate the reaction and keep enough tension in the connector to maintain control.

Another interesting aspect of impact training was learning how to strike and control the rebound directions of targets that were distorted (not even or symmetrical in inherent shape or configuration) or interrupted in anatomical form. These types of striking techniques were usually the last to be learned since there were so many possible angles, directions, and positions that the adversary could take during an actual confrontation.

By the time the ninja had reached a plateau of proficiency in impact training, he had usually begun more intense phases of development that involved applying fighting theory. Since articulated warfare varied enormously from fixed weapon combat, he had to learn the similarities and differences between the two. This took the guidance and expertise of a senior operative who had acquired actual experience in life-or-death situations to tutor him in this art.

He was first taught the major theoretical differences between offensive and defensive tactics. For instance, in cases

The chigi-riki could be used to capture and incapacitate an unsuspecting opponent's weapon.

where the enemy would initiate the first attack, it was always better to intercept, block, or evade the assault first rather than attempt the risky business of trying to get an offensive technique in before the attack struck. With articulated weapons, the most common defensive tactic was that of counterattacking with "stop-hit" types of ploys. The stop-hit counterattack was one of the ways in which the beater, chain connector, or staff handle was used to block or intercept the oncoming attack while an effort was made to follow up with a simultaneous counterattack. To fully appreciate this combination tactic, the *chigi-riki* technician had to learn evasive footwork while accurately and unconsciously remaining acutely alert to the opponent's tricks and obvious tactical intentions.

Offensively, the ninja had many techniques and stratagems at his disposal. Within the realm of stealth methodology, trickery, diversion, fakes, feints, redirection strikes, reaps, lasso maneuvers, the use of other objects to throw at the enemy while executing his attack, and radical and unpredictable range variations (for which the *chigi-riki* was ideally suited), all worked very well with the wide assortment of offensive techniques he learned during his tenure as a novice ninja operative.

Though every combative engagement would undoubtedly be different, while learning fighting theory the ninja also learned to rely quite heavily on his instincts and the use of the five elements of universal harmony—these being *ku* (the emptiness), *fu* (the wind), *ka* (the fire), *sui* (the water), and *chi* (the earth). Each of these levels expressed and emphasized a different method of dealing with every part of the ninja's daily life, including actual combat situations. Sometimes this wisdom took years to acquire, fully comprehend, and then incorporate into his fighting style.

As his familiarity of the theoretical uses of the *chigi-riki*, expanded,the ninja's primary concern became learning all of the positions in which the weapon could be held at the different ranges (long-, mid-, and close-range respectively). First and foremost in this phase of training was acquiring the actual ready-fighting attitudes the cornered ninja needed when squared off with an enemy intent on taking his life. These body postures and corresponding grips were similar to the "on-guard" positions used in the European art of fencing. However, because of the complexities of articulated weapons, there were many more deceptive ways to position the *chigi-riki*.

One of the main drawbacks to using flexible weapons was that the weapon itself could not adequately provide full protection in the preparatory positions. What it lacked in that

Here the chigi-riki is used to entangle the opponent's legs and drop him to the ground.

respect it more than made up for in ready fighting positions from which swift and forceful defensive stop-hit strikes and counterattacks could be made. When the ninja practiced with a training partner who assumed the role of an enemy, he learned to use positioning and the five elements to guide him in the appropriate attitudes to assume against a given type of weapon or weapon-wielding adversary.

The elusive *shinobi* assassins of Japan had an unquenchable desire to master a weapon and its use. Delving into every conceivable facet of weapon-tool usage became almost an obsession with these phantoms of darkness.This being the case, the *chigi-riki* practitioner set out to master the attitudes of wielding the weapon through a wide range of one- and two-handed attitudes. The two-handed attitudes were considered to be the power techniques, whereas single-handed manipulations stressed speed.

Because the *chigi-riki* could be disguised as a cane when the chain connector was secretly stowed inside the hollow handle, the ninja devised ingenious extraction methods using two hands. Using one hand to push the force of the hidden chain out of the tubular confinement while the other pulled the rear portion of the staff was a highly exacting skill. It had to be powerful and accurately timed for distance and trajectory so the beater would strike the intended target without warning.

If the *chigi-riki* was a fixed type on which the chain was mounted to the end of the hand staff, two-handed gripping methods were much more complex. Among the unorthodox techniques learned later in the training were holding the soft or taut chain (or beater) in one hand while the other retained a portion of the hand staff or holding the chain and beater and using the hand staff as the beater.

More basic maneuvers taught in this phase of training included directional attitudes, versatility for sudden redirecting, oblique striking and blocking, power-oriented techniques that individually or in combination included these offensive-defensive movements, two-handed feed-out maneuvers in which range was altered to shift from power to speed mode, and a wide variety of specialized techniques where inherent feel and motion were essential to their effectiveness. The one-handed speed-oriented techniques were then introduced. In many cases the speed associated with these maneuvers was what kept the chain taut and provided it with the characteristics of a fixed weapon, at least up until the beater or chain struck the target. Some of the common one-handed techniques included figure eights, elliptical twirls, whip-strikes, reaps, lasso looping, javelin-style spearing (in which the chain and beater were held in one hand for close-range striking while the other hand was used to restrain or control the enemy, or when it was preoccupied performing another function such as climbing), and distracting the opponent with *metsubushi*, *shuriken*, or the like. Another unique one-handed maneuver (though it may seem like a two-handed one) was coiling the chain connector while the weapon was in motion, then suddenly unleashing it when the time was right to injure or incapacitate the enemy. Naturally, the ninja operative learned to use both hands with equal dexterity even though he may have only needed one to perform a certain type of offensive or defensive technique.

The strike-to-attitude relationships, which normally followed this extensive regimen of *chigi-riki* training, in most cases, overlapped the circular and figure-eight attitudes. Simultaneously adjusting the body's physical positioning to complement the type of technique that was being executed proved to be a valuable asset to any ninja operative using articulated weaponry. Allowing for the body to subtly move out of the way as a spinning or circling chain came hurling from behind him, or maneuvering under, over, or around the weapon's arc while evading and counterattacking an armed assailant were also among the many ruses the *shinobi* operative could perform with uncanny proficiency when he had mastered this difficult phase of training.

Visual considerations were not normally associated with shorter-range fixed weapons used by the ninja, but they were of prime importance when dealing with the awkward and cumbersome articulated combat implements. Primarily because a spinning chain and beater required space, it was essential to have unobstructed access to an enemy's vital targets and keep a sharp eye on the opponent and the spatial boundaries at the same time without becoming totally preoccupied with this constantly changing situation. This required the ability to scan the environment and automatically know what techniques were applicable in a given situation.

Of course, as the relationship of movement between the ninja and the enemy changed from moment to moment while embroiled in combat, the ninja had to be able to adapt his strategy and techniques without interrupting or taking his eyes off of his opponent. This skill was acquired after many sessions of mock combat with a competent trainer who intentionally created situations to test the visual considerations of his student. Once the *chigi-riki* proponent had mastered this stage of training, his peripheral vision and strike-to-attitude relationships improved considerably. These qualities were also necessary when using many of the other weapon-tools in the ninja arsenal.

Mastering this ultimately led to the ninja *chigi-riki* expert's merging any and all of the offensive-defensive and recovery techniques that he had learned during his training with the weapon. This, in turn, prepared him for actually putting it to use against an unsuspecting enemy who had the unfortunate fate of meeting the *shinobi* assassin in a bout of mortal combat, where the outcome was usually determined by the one who had learned his weapon skills well and was willing to pay the price for a fatal mistake. The feudal age ninja operative was willing to do both with great pride and determination.

Chapter Seven

FISTLOAD WEAPONRY

The infamous ninja clan members of feudal Japan were creators and advocates of weapon-tools that served as both agricultural implements and weapons in times of crisis. In many instances, acts of espionage and subversion were directly responsible for the original adaptation of these unique martial innovations, much like the western world's concept of necessity as the mother of invention.

Improvisation of such seemingly simple yet awesome weapon-tools took many shapes and forms. Some incorporat-

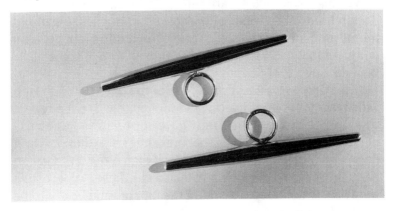

The shobo was only one of the many fistload weapons employed by the ninja. It was versatile because of the ring or loop attached near the middle of each shank.

Different forms of makeshift fistload weapons employed by the feudal-age ninja assassins.

ed staffs of various shapes and dimensions; chains, ropes and leather cords; bladed spades and other digging implements; harvesting tools such as large and small scythes; cutlery; utilitarian hardware; livestock harnesses; common household items used during that time; and even crude pieces of iron and steel that had long been cast aside in favor of some other manufactured tool.

The *shinobi-shobo*, a short shank of rounded wood or iron with a leather or iron ring (finger loop) attached to the center, was one of these unassuming weapons. It is generally believed that the *shobo* was the forerunner of the *kakute* (iron rings with protruding spikes) and *tekken* (an ornamental metal band that slipped over the foreknuckles). These two weapons were considered predecessors of the first brass knuckles to be used in Japan.

Again, as with many other ninja weapon-tools, agricultural functions played a vital role in their original inception. The

Not all fistloads were made of metal. This spiked version was fashioned from a short piece of wood.

Another improvised fistload made out of hand-forged metal.

A spine dagger fistload used by the ninja. This deadly spike was usually used by the female ninja operative after she put her victim in an uncompromising amorous position. She would then remove it from her hair and swiftly force it into the base of the samurai's brain.

shobo is thought to have derived from that origin as well. Agriculturally, there were numerous common uses for short wooden or metal staves and shanks. Early bridle bits for horses and livestock, harness rings used for connecting reins and yokes, metal or wood hinge pins for gates or doors, pulley swivel pins for water well mechanisms, and bolts for locking closures were among the most common functions of such a simple, yet necessary, item.

The ninja, by nature of their inherited vocation as stealth operatives, learned at a very early age that adaptation played an important role in their and the entire clan's survival, and duplicity was an integral part of that coexistence while living in harmony with nature. Other than their immediate family, religious convictions, and moral edicts, there was no item or thing so sanctimonious (as opposed to the beliefs of their arch rivals the samurai warriors) that it could not be used for more than one specific purpose. This demonstrates why the mountain mystics were so skilled at constructing or inventing functional items from others that were originally intended for another use. Based upon this logic, the *shinobi-shobo* could have been made from any of the common stavelike items present in Japan during the feudal age.

By basic design, the *shobo*, when adapted militarily, possessed many close-range fistload characteristics. Most were intended to be used to enhance, strengthen, or fortify the empty-hand fighting methodology stressed in *tai-jutsu* tactics.

As a short section of usually round tapered wood or iron shank, the *shobo* ranged in length from about 7 inches to over 11 inches. Affixed to its middle was a ring or finger loop that could be swiveled depending upon the diameter of the hole

Though a fistload lacked the range of many traditional ninja weapons, it was still an effective deterrent in the hands of a skilled operative. Here the adversary is wielding a weighted chain; the ninja is armed only with a set of ringed shobo.

The ninja strikes his opponent's lead hand with the pointed shank of the shobo.

The pain forces the opponent to momentarily cease his aggressiveness. This is the split second that the shinobi needs to launch his attack by thrusting the pointed end of the weapon into his opponent's eyes.

in the shaft relative to the thickness of the cord or metal pin. The hand-forged riveted finger ring of the metal varieties were generally loose enough to spin freely when it was not firmly gripped in the wielder's hand. Depending on the personal preferences of its maker, the ninja clan member could opt to increase the lethality of his *shobo* by beveling or forging the metal ends until they were very sharp.

As a fistload (short hand-held fist-fortifying weapon), the *shobo* worked very efficiently when its inherent weaponlike qualities were synthesized with the refined close-range fighting arts of *tai-jutsu*. Since *tai-jutsu* included highly exacting techniques in striking, blocking, *jutai-jutsu* (grappling), choking, strangulation, escaping holds, *taihenjutsu* (silent movement when stalking a prey or escaping), rolling, leaping, and tumbling, one or two could be used with ease without hampering the complete use of the ninja's hands.

As the shadow warrior became adept at wielding the weapon in these fashions, natural progression usually led him to mastering a variety of specialized techniques in which the *shobo* was used in even more crucial ways. These techniques included augmented or reinforced blocking maneuvers where the small sections of wood or metal were placed precisely to intercept or deflect a powerful weapon blow without harming the user.

When the *shobo* was used solely for such defensive purposes, however, it lacked severely. For that reason the ninja had to rely strongly on evasive tactics, in the form of side stepping, ducking, dodging, leaping over, diving under, or swiftly intercepting an antagonist's weapon or extremity attack before the full force of the assault struck him. In some defensive cases, his own *tai-jutsu* blocks could suffice to defend against nonbladed weapons before vicious and aggressive *shobo* attack techniques were brought into play.

The true advantages of the *shobo* were seen in its close-range offensive mode. These techniques included reinforced strikes with the pointed ends directed to the eyes, ear cavities, temple, and base of the skull; puncturing the brain through the nostrils; powerful thrusting jabs into the front of the neck; and forceful penetration over, under, around (and, in some opportune instances, through) the ribs to rupture the vital organs. When a wire or thin strong cord was attached between the rings, a very effective garrote was created. This form of *tai-jutsu* combined with *taihenjutsu* made an ideal weapon for eliminating or silencing an unsuspecting sentry guarding a bastion or stronghold.

Other *tai-jutsu* and *shobo* methodology could be found in the wide assortment of close-range offensive techniques the ninja used to momentarily inflict excruciating pain on an antagonist who tried to capture him. Virtually every part of the *shobo* could be used with equal effectiveness to attack vulnerable pressure points, sensitive areas under the ear, in the armpit cavity, behind the thorax, at most of the points along the inner joints, and even the groin. These were all essential techniques for breaking restraint while temporarily disabling the enemy just enough to finish him off or escape.

As with most ninja tactics, many of the *shobo* close-range fighting and escaping methods were kept secret. To one not so knowledgeable of the many unique ways that it could be used in empty-hand combat, the short length of staff with a finger ring represented little more than a hand-held truncheon. Simply put, it seemed as if it were capable of basic short club strikes that could only inflict superficial damage. Most skeptics usually found out too late that there was more than one way to grip or hold the *shobo*. That is why there were so many types of grips that were essential for the ninja to master if the weapon was going to be used to its fullest potential. It is also why the ninja valued secrecy and never revealed their techniques except to a trusted and privileged few within the immediate clan. These were normally brothers and sisters of members of the clan who had been raised together since childhood.

These gripping methods had many fighting advantages. Rather than the obvious basic strikes and reinforced punching methods evident with any fistload weapon, the swivel

The ninja shuriken (throwing star) could also suffice as a fistload. Careful placement in the palm with a firm grip made this clever technique possible.

combined with various fingers inserted through the ring created some rather unobvious yet very lethal possibilities when it was wielded by one so gifted with the knowledge and wisdom of their insidious applications. Much depended on the directional attitude of the hand placement and the degree of opening of the hand.

Some of the fundamental unorthodox techniques made possible by the less obvious gripping methods were powerful bone-crushing attacks to the bridge of the nose, frontal lobe, and base of the skull, and even strikes where the pointed *shobo* could actually crush, penetrate, and instantly pierce the heart or lungs through the rib cage. The instant shock combined with the immediate loss of large amounts of blood was enough to fell even the most determined opponents. In some cases, some of these very same alternative-grip techniques could be used to penetrate light armor and still inflict the same lethality.

The real versatility of combining *tai-jutsu* methodology and exacting gripping styles came when the experienced *shobo* exponent could perform them simultaneously in a dexterous manner, all while engaged in a bout of heated combat where his or his adversary's life was at stake. This talent—combined with the unusual assortment of special techniques that included raking, gouging, ripping, and controlling an enemy's movement and actions—definitely made the ninja a force to be reckoned with, even against a weapon-wielding foe who was equally skilled with his own sword, staff, or halberd.

To accomplish these seemingly impossible feats against an armed enemy, the ninja also had to rely quite heavily on many other skills he achieved through years of rigorous combat training. These skills included human qualities like precise timing; agility; balance; instant reactionary response to the enemy's movement; reading his intentions; knowing when to attack rather than evade a cut or slash; deception induced through *seishin teki kyoyo* (spiritual refinement); his

What may appear to be a ninja operative performing a jumon spell-casting ritual is actually misleading. A shobo concealed in the closed palms is ready to be brought into action. This was a typical tactic used when the ninja was cornered and outnumbered by enemy forces.

own experiential knowledge in practiced *bo-jutsu* (stick and staff fighting), *yari-jutsu* (spear fighting), *naginata-jutsu* (halberd fighting), *kusarigama-jutsu* (chain and sickle arts), and *bo-*

ryaku (strategy); and a committed *kyojitsu tenkan ho* philosophy where survival and accomplishment meant more to him than the risk of engaging an adversary.

To combine all of these human and emotional qualities in the exact amounts to suit a particular criteria meant the ninja warrior had to spend years in intense training with the *shobo*. Once he had mastered it, then and only then did he fully understand the full potential that he held in his hand. It was also a paramount moment when the shadow warrior had acquired a fuller appreciation of the other less combative, yet just as important, functions that his ring-looped fistload could perform during emergencies.

By its simple design, when cords were connected to one or more of them, the *shobo* could be converted into a weapon-tool similar to the cleats (pitons) used for climbing up the faces of mountains. This same technique could be used equally as well for scaling castle walls or other craggy obstacles where the pointed ends of the *shobo* could be inserted. Once he had ascended to a higher level, he could jerk free the connecting cords and duplicate the process until he reached the top.

The use of the ring as a tying point for cords and ropes also made it somewhat suited as a quasi grappling hook. This simplified conversion made it possible to hurl the rope-connected *shobo* high into a tree or other exposed crevice. Once the shaft had been set or trapped firmly between two open abutments, the ninja could climb the rope just as if it were a regular grappling hook. By not having curved prongs, it was usually easier to disengage than the typical ones, but it lacked their full capability as well.

As with many of the original utilitarian functions any short section of rounded or tapered shank served, the *shobo* was always as useful as it ever was. One example of a tool application was the way it could be used as a pry bar. This was accomplished by inserting the shank into an opening and using a lever bar stuck into the ring. Gates, doors, windows, or the like could be forced open in this manner. As a makeshift lock pick, the *shobo* could be jammed forcefully into a simple mechanism. Then with a strong blow with another object, the pins of the locking mechanism could be bent so that the lock opened. Chiseling, hammering, wedging, and jamming doors or entrance openings could be performed in a similar manner. When the *shobo* was wedged into a door jamb, it could prevent any pursuing enemy from opening it as he made good his escape from a castle.

There were many ways to grip the *shinobi-shobo*, and each revealed certain inherent *tai-jutsu* fighting characteristics that were only known by the ninja operative. Not only did he have to know how to wield it for each style of fighting, but he had to be equally skilled at maneuvering the *shobo* from one grip to

GRIPPING THE SHINOBI-SHOBO

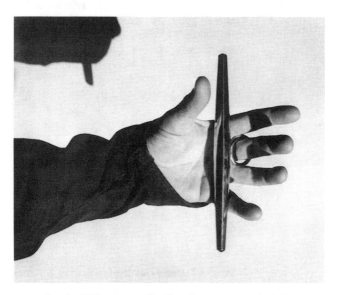

Open hand middle ring push grip. *This grip was used when angulated driving force was needed to strike a pressure point or vital organ. The thumb plus the secured retention of the ring made this possible. Notice that the open hand could also be used to grab or restrain an enemy or his weapon while the gouging or pushing techniques were occurring.*

Closed fist middle ring outside grip. *This grip was used in much the same fashion as brass knuckles or other fistloads where the face of the fist had to be reinforced. By releasing the tension on the fingers and flicking the wrist, the ninja could convert the pointed ends of the shobo into a spearlike weapon for striking other difficult-to-reach targets such as the the neck. When positioned to the side or rear of his adversary, he could also execute eye-raking techniques.*

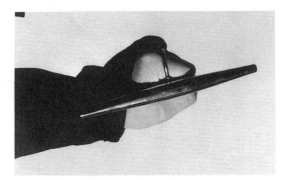

Closed fist middle ring inside grip. *This grip provided the shinobi with additional striking capabilities with the protruding spikes at each end of the hand. Though they did not penetrate as well as some of the other spear strikes, they were highly effective for the eyes, temple, pressure points, and ear cavities. The clinched fist also strengthened other parts of the hand when punching or other common fist-striking techniques were used.*

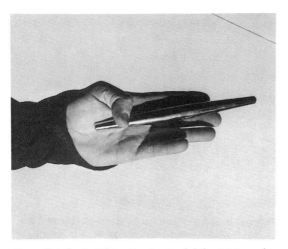

Spear hand grip. *The spear grip extended the ninja's reach by several inches. In addition to fortifying the fingers used in many spear hand strikes, open-palm slapping and raking techniques could be applied at extremely close ranges.*

Double hand ring grip. *This grip was used when powerful leverage or thrusting techniques were needed. By simply removing one hand from the shobo, the ninja could also convert to several other grips.*

Teppo grip. *This grip was known as the teppo (iron rod) grip and was used predominately for lunging strikes to the inside of an adversary's middle or in lateral circular attacks to the outside of his fighting position. When stealth attacks were executed from the rear of an adversary, the shaft of the shobo could be driven into the teeth or bridge of the nose, or it could assist in strangulation techniques when the other hand was used to apply the choking force.*

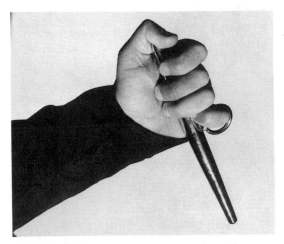

End ring dagger grip. *This grip positioned the fistload in much the same fashion as a dagger or other bladed instrument for stabbing, ripping, or gouging targets where great amounts of overhead force were needed to achieve deep penetration.*

Two-finger grip. *This specialty grip was used predominantly as a means for the ninja to execute two-finger eye pokes without having to use both hands. Though this could be done fairly well using only one hand with two real fingers, the shinobi preferred to use his "iron finger" instead. The results were obviously more effective.*

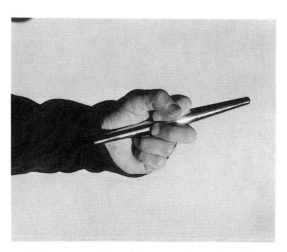

Scorpion grip. *This grip was sometimes known as the "monkey fist" because of the many unique ways it could be manipulated to block, strike, poke, gouge, rip, punch, and dig.*

Spider grip. This grip was used in blocks and other open-hand techniques where simultaneous striking was needed. It was among the most common gripping methods for offensive and defensive close-range fighting techniques.

Staff grip. Although the finger was not placed through the ring, this grip was still effective for most techniques where end strikes or punching manuevers were employed. Because the finger was not put through the ring, the ninja could readily change the shobo to the other hand rather than change his fighting posture.

another as the situation dictated. He had to do this swiftly and smoothly if he was going to use his weapon with optimum effectiveness.

Chapter Eight

INVISIBILITY WEAPONRY

Throughout the annals of feudal Japan, much has been recorded about the infamous ninja's ability to seemingly vanish into thin air. This feat conjured up images of mystical demons or superhuman beings who possessed the uncanny ability to disappear suddenly and reappear at will, even in the confining environs where capture was inevitable by their arch enemies, the samurai vassals of an opposing faction of his secret clients! They, like many other unenlightened people of Japan's ancient past, failed to fully realize the potential uses of the elements of nature and the mystical and oftentimes strategic advantages these elusive shadow warriors could create from these natural elements.

Metsubushi, the ninja's phantom art of invisibility, was much more than a mere way of vanishing when he was outnumbered or discovered by an enemy bent on capturing him after he had infiltrated a warlord's stronghold. It was a highly exacting science based on a deep understanding of many natural, logical (and sometimes illogical), and tactical phenomena.

Whereas most skeptical individuals would try to explain the *shinobi's* ability to perform such vanishing acts as mere trickery, others based these wizards' ghostlike ruses on their ability to communicate with the spirit world, almost as if they had reached a plateau of enlightenment where their sorcererlike manifestations could be called upon instantly when needed. Naturally, one had to be within a higher realm to produce such astounding miracles. Little did each faction know how right they both were!

In actuality, the *shinobi* operative based many of his or her mental and spiritual abilities on the secret knowledge found within the doctrines of the *mikkyo*, which was wisdom stemming from the teachings found in the ancient scrolls of Tibetan Tantric lore. These sacred books taught that all physical aspects of existence originated from the same source and could be classified into one of five manifestations of the elements:

Ku—the emptiness, or the source of subatomic energy, the nothing from which all things take their form.

Fu—the wind, or elements in a gaseous state.

Ka—the fire, or elements in an energy releasing state.

Sui—the water, or elements in a fluid state.

Chi—the earth, or elements in a solid state.

Because of their strong religious belief and deeper ways of perceiving reality, their *yamabushi* (warrior mountain priest) teachings gave them many ways of accomplishing difficult tasks that would have been virtually impossible without knowledge of the options or solutions dictated by these Tibetan doctrines. This knowledge was little known and rarely understood by those who had not been raised within the secretive ninja clans.

Even from the physical standpoint, the ninja operative was taught from a very early age that the Tibetan Tantric lore could be applied to situations where the actual elements (wind, fire, water, earth) could be used separately or harmoniously to create a medium in which tactical stratagems could be developed. Many of these ingenious techniques were found in the 18 levels of training that a ninja received during his or her apprenticeship toward becoming a full-fledged *shinobi* shadow warrior.

To fully appreciate the combination of wisdom and physical skills possessed by the feudal-age ninja, one had to think in a like manner. This is perhaps best expressed in the ingeniously creative ways that the *shinobi* made use of natural elements within his environment. The cunning ways that they could be adapted to create illusions and foster seemingly superhuman feats further strengthened the air of mysticism that surrounded the *shinobi's* deceptive and secretive lives.

The *metsubushi* and the art of using blinding concoctions was only one of the fighting tools employed by the ninja to perform such impossible feats as disappearing before an enemy's eyes. As within the tenets found within the *mikkyo* book of secret knowledge, there was always more than one way to accomplish or approach a given situation.

The ninja had several options at his disposal with the art of "vanishing," or using cleverly contrived methods of making the enemy think that he had disappeared. Among them were using the elements of nature in the strictest sense. The *gotonpo* (five elements of escape) within the 18 levels of ninja training taught them that the natural elements of earth, water, fire, metal, and wood, when used appropriately, could create the illusion of disappearing.

By appearing as, simulating, or blending with an element at the right time and in the proper environment, his existence became virtually undetectable. This disappearing feat could be accomplished, for example, by submerging under water using an apparatus such as a reed or underwater breathing tube. Likewise, wearing the proper attire to blend with the environment and camouflage his presence, burying himself under the earth for extended periods of time until danger had passed, dashing into fires while wearing protective garments, starting fires and then being consumed by them using the same technique, assuming the identity of another person, and seemingly disappearing into thin air by using ropes and portable self-contained ladders were all ways in which the elements of *goton-po* could be adapted to the elusive phantom's needs.

The art of *metsubushi* (sight removers or eye blinders) was an alternate approach to accomplishing miraculous vanishing feats. Since options always played a vital role in the ninja's clandestine life, rather than deceiving an adversary into assuming that he had disappeared by using *goton-po* methodology, the ninja could use alternate techniques to vanish.

One of the vanishing acts of the ninja required the use of smoke bombs and a grappling hook. Once the smoke had spread thick and dense, the ninja used his kagi-nawa to ascend into a tree or other high perch.

Whether the enemy could not see because of camouflage or because he had temporarily or permanently lost his vision to an insidious concoction of *metsubushi*, it was the ninja's reasoning that they both served the same purpose in the end.

The art of making and using sight removers and blinding concoctions was a highly guarded secret for many centuries. There were many secret formulas and diverse ways that these irritating substances could be dispersed. Another important aspect, though not as critical, was the means by which these sight removers could be contained before or during the expelling process.

Among the most common substances used to make *met-subushi* blinding and irritating agents was a wide assortment of hot peppers. Many came from the solanaceous plant of the genus capsicum. The pungent seeds of these podded or bell-shaped pericarps could be ground into a fine powder with a mortar and pestle or other makeshift powdering device. Even two flat stones worked exceedingly well in converting the dried seeds to flour.

Other just as potent extractions could be derived in this fashion from the plants, stalks, roots, and seeds of the solanums, belladonna, henbane, mandrake, and tobacco tubers, some of which the Portuguese introduced in the mid-1400s. With crude forms of distillation, liquids and crystallized forms of these irritants could be produced and stored until needed for a mission.

With the ninja's pharmaceutical skills, he could concoct many types of blinding, poisonous, and explosive mixtures. These lethal formulas were placed in nut shells and thrown into fires or directly into the enemy's face.

The alchemy know-how possessed by the ninja was equally effective in producing *metsubushi* from many other sources. Grinding up certain organs from lizards, frogs, venomous spiders, dead animals that had putrefied (from which putrescine, or liquid ptomaine, could be extracted), and fish that carried sacs of poison to protect themselves was a way to produce the vile and very toxic powdered or liquefied derivatives.

Metsubushi mixtures were also housed in eggshells.

Other less potent irritants could be contrived and used as *metsubushi* from mixtures of fine grit, ashes that had been mixed with finely powdered peppers, nettle hairs from plants, caustic potash, pulverized volcanic glass pumice, and certain herbs that contained mild irritants. Depending upon the purpose, since some of the more deadly extractions could also be used as poisons on the *fuki-ya* (darts) for the *fukedake* (blowgun), the ninja operative may have opted to soak nonlethal agents with these mixtures to give them added weight and even greater effective range. Naturally, this was all at the discretion of the *shinobi* operative and the type of mission he was on.

Containments, being the packets in which the blinders and sight removers were kept, were as many and varied as the *metsubushi* themselves, ranging from simple folded paper wrappers to larger, more sturdy nut shells. Among the variations in between were split walnut hulls that were emptied and refilled with *metsubushi*, hollowed eggshells with wax plugs to encapsulate the blinding powders, hollow canes or sword scabbards that could be filled and flicked into the enemy's face, and *metsubushi* boxes with storage cavities that resembled small, ornate opium pipes. When the enemy was in close proximity, the operative simply removed the plug and blew the *metsubushi* out of the spout end and into the direction of his pursuer.

Other improvised items found their way into the ninja's canister arsenal as well. These included small fragile porcelain containers that broke easily on contact, hollow parchment wrappers that burned rapidly and released the irritants into the air of an enemy camp, and delicate hollow baked clay spheres that could be used in much the same fashion once the container broke.

With the availability of black powder and other slow-burn-

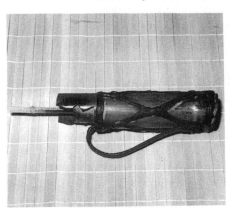

This ornate device gave the ninja the ability to incapacitate an unsuspecting enemy with one breath. With the plug pulled, the mouthpiece permitted a forceful blow of air to send a cloud of metsubushi powder out the front and into the eyes of a pursuer. These devices later found their way into police use to subdue unruly suspects during Japan's Tokugawa era.

ing explosives, the ninja operatives devised sophisticated ways in which the irritants and explosives could be combined. This actually increased the volatile potential of the *metsubushi* while adding another surprising dimension to their ability to vanish in a cloud of smoke. A blinding black pepper combined with a thundering boom and thick blackish-gray smoke not only stunned and temporarily blinded but disoriented the unsuspecting antagonist as well, thus enabling the shrewd *shinobi* to vanish.

The *goton-po* and knowledge of the Tibetan Tantric lore's *mikkyo* (secret knowledge) played a vital role in providing the ninja with the many means in which to release the *metsubushi* onto an enemy. By using the five elements—Ku (the emptiness), Fu (the wind), Ka (the fire), Sui (the water), and Chi (the earth)—as methods of divine guidance, the ninja could determine the options of how to actually dispense the *metsubushi* blinding agents.

These five methods likewise could take many specific forms. For instance, if the breath was used to blow a blinding powder into the face of an adversary (representing the element of Fu), this could be performed by use of the mouth only or through a *fukedake*. Shape or form were inconsequential as long as the means suited the specific purpose. Any device, regardless of how abstract or illogical, would be used to defeat an adversary if that's what it took to complete an assigned mission. A simple blowgun arrangement, where wind was blown through a tube, may have taken the form of a flute, a hollow tube used for breathing under water, a hollow walking cane, the *saya* (scabbard) used to sheath his sword, or simply his mouth. The essence of the disbursement method was really in the element used to provide the propulsion. In the case of Fu it was the breath.

There was a handful of methods to expel or propel the *metsubushi* potions. Self-contamination (extract of the earth element) was one method that actually let the enemy contaminate his own eyes. This could be accomplished with either the liquid or powdered varieties.

The feudal age ninja was well versed in conscious (intentional) and unconscious (unintentional) behavioral patterns of individuals. Involuntary and voluntary human responses also fit into this area of *bo-ryaku* (strategy). By knowing that within a given period of time a person could be expected to subconsciously put his fingers or hands in the vicinity of his nose or face, the ninja could be fairly certain that if a powered or liquid *metsubushi* was unknowingly placed on his hands, it would eventually come in contact with his eyes. The ninja could perform this unconventional means of transferring an eye irritant to a sentry or the like by observing his mannerisms and seeing what he touched. Then he would stealthfully sprinkle the potion on those objects, and then it was just a matter of time until the *metsubushi* worked its way up to its intended target.

In many cases this stratagem was a delayed tactic, but it was quite effective at inducing misery and temporary blindness and at least giving the shadow warrior enough time to escape detection. This same self-contamination ruse had many other applications within the realm of stealth, and the deceptive ninja knew how to apply them extremely well under a given set of circumstances.

A *ninja operative disperses mitsubushi sight removers with his hand.*

Hand propulsion (extract of the metal element) was most typically associated with the way that the *shinobi* warrior pulled off a vanishing act. It was direct, bold, unexpected, highly calculated, and immediate, especially if he was cornered or trapped by one or more adversaries during a mission.

In this realm of using the elements to guide his actions, the ninja operative relied quite heavily on physical attributes such as accuracy, speed, judgment of distances, etc. to hurl the containers or loose powders into the enemy's face. Several *metsubushi*-filled eggshells or the like, quickly and accurately thrown, were usually all that was needed to blind a pursuing enemy long enough for the ninja to make good his escape.

Breath propulsion (extract of the wind element) was another

A shinobi warrior blows a thick cloud of metsubushi directly into the face of an oncoming enemy.

way to expel irritants. The ninja used his breath and lung power for many things. Blowing darts, emulating the sounds of birds and animals as signals, playing musical instruments when disguised as a traveling musician, and remaining submerged under water for extended periods of time were all ways in which he used his breath to carry out his stealthful craft.

In addition to the previously mentioned ways that the wind element was used to expel *metsubushi*, the cunning *shinobi* operative could use it to propel blinding powders through smoking pipes or long reeds secretly inserted into rooms where the enemy was sleeping, or blow it into the wind so it would travel in the direction of an enemy encampment. In this manner, he could disburse the powders over a broad range and affect many people simultaneously.

The use of water pressure (extract of the water element) as a method of propelling liquid irritants was perhaps considerably more effective at the greater ranges than the air pressure methods. Whereas the breath could be used at ranges of up to approximately 40 feet (unless expelled in the same direction the wind was blowing), the water propulsion methods were fairly accurate up to 60 to 70 feet.

These water-powered devices were known as "poison water guns" and consisted of a large hollow tube in which a smaller plungerlike ramrod was inserted. A liquid poison was poured into the mouth of the outer tube and plugged with beeswax or other waterproof wadding. In some cases, a small hole was drilled in the joint section of a bamboo shaft in much the same fashion as a modern toy water gun. When the liquid was compressed with the hand-operated plunger, the *metsubushi* was expelled in a small forceful stream. This technique was later used with flammable liquids and as an alternate method of shooting poisoned missiles and darts.

Explosive propulsion (extract of the fire element) was a later development. As the use of black powder and other slow-burning explosives became more prevalent in feudal Japan, the ninja soon devised many ways in which they could be incorporated into their weapon-tool arsenal. Adapting them to use with powdered or liquefied *metsubushi* was among the more unique ways of applying this technology. Since Ka represented the gaseous state, and since rapidly heated explosives expanded at a rate in proportion to the amount used and how tightly it was contained, there were many viable applications for disbursing *metsubushi*.

Among these shrewdly contrived devices were smoke bombs, exploding capsules, projectiles that broke open on impact and released their contents, containers of metal filings and other small objects that had been soaked in liquefied *metsubushi*, and even small grenadelike viles that exploded and released the eye irritants when secretly tossed into an enemy's encampment fire. All were designed to surprise, blind, and confuse the unsuspecting enemy.

****

With the knowledge of how to make, encapsulate, and disburse the many forms of liquid and powdered *metsubushi*, a *shinobi* operative became an even more feared rival. This skill earned him the infamous reputation as an elusive phantom, thus proliferating the legend that this mystical magician was indeed a ghost who had attained the enlightened state of invisibility.

Chapter Nine
SPIKE WEAPONRY

Tetsubishi iron-spiked caltrops were among the many "nuisance" weapons found in the shadow warrior's awesome *tonki* or *toniki* personal arsenal. Also included in the *tonki* category was a substantial array of annoyance-invoking instruments such as throwing spikes and bladed stars (*shuriken*) and various configurations of dirks, double-edged daggers, stilleto-like shivs, and knife-type sundries. All were capable of inflicting various degrees of injury depending on how they were used and who was wielding them.

The *tetsubishi* was only one of these insidiously clever weapons. Although it was considered by many noted weapon historians to be more of a nuisance tool than a real deadly threat, it was still deemed an essential item that the ninja operative routinely kept in his bag or secret pockets along with more lethal devices, primarily because they provided him with strategic options not normally available with many of the other pouch-stored weapon-tools in his possession.

The *tetsubishi* derived its origin from nature. It was a by-product of various plants having spiny heads of fruit from which the name "caltrops" was derived. Most of these Old World plants were of the genera tribulus and kallstroemia or trapa natans. The latter was commonly referred to as the "water chestnut" or "water caltrop" because of the shape of its dried aquatic fruit once the outer shells had hardened after being exposed to the sun for extended periods of time.

The ninja, like so many early societies, saw the distinct military advantages of these multipointed pericarps. In feudal times, dried water chestnuts and crude metal facsimiles

Standard iron tetsubishi were among the most infamous ninja "nuisance" weapons.

resembling iron balls with four projecting spikes were used to obstruct foot soldiers and armored vehicles drawn by horses, and to incapacitate scantily shod enemies in pursuit of fleeing ninja rivals. These tactical ruses were made possible because the weapon was disposed in such a manner that one of the four sharp spikes was always pointed upward when the caltrop was dispensed.

As a *tonki* spiked weapon, the ninja referred to the earlier dried chestnut versions as *hishi-bishi*, or "natural caltrops." They also placed a great deal of importance on it as a food source to sustain them while on long-distance espionage missions. The *hishi*, being a harvested staple crop throughout the rural farming areas of Japan, was ideally suited as a food supplement since it grew in the remote areas where many of the clandestine ninja clans lived. After harvesting the abundant quantities of water chestnuts, the peasant farmers, many of whom were secret ninja cult members, placed the green and nearly ripe water caltrops in the sun for several months until the shells were shriveled and drawn and the four thorny protrusions were pronounced. Sometimes, to speed up the process, they exposed the drying fruit to low heat over an open hearth until the outer shells had hardened and took on the appearance and feel of burnished iron. Although no two water chestnut shells were identical in form or shape, these unique *tennenbishi* sharp points generally formed in such a way that each spike protruded in a different direction. With the moisture content dissipated, the fruit dried to a rock-hard state and the pericarp points tempered like seasoned steel. The ingenious *ninpo* operatives had both preserved a food stuff and created an abundant supply of *hishi-bishi* for operational purposes.

The ninja's fascination with this process was undoubtedly responsible for their inventing their own caltrops. These were

A *collection of ingenious homemade ninja caltrops.*

given the name of *tetsubishi,* or iron caltrops.

As with the earlier form of darts (*fukiya*) made of dried bones, thistles, or the like, and *shuriken* (throwing blades) made of stone, the ninja's experimentation with iron and various semihardened metals provided them with a deeper insight into the military and tactical advantages of such malleable substances. Though nature could always be relied upon to provide necessary backup materials for weapon-tools, the specialized manufacture of such lethal instruments tended to elevate their effectiveness and ultimately enable the *shinobi* assassin to perform a task or carry out a clandestine mission in a much more efficient manner. This was the case as the ninja gradually switched from the *hishi-bishi* natural water chestnut caltrops to the even more lethal *tetsubishi* metal fabricated ones.

Among the first true *tetsubishi* devised by the early ninja clans were versions that actually preceded the metal varieties. The *kobishi* wooden triangle was made out of solid sections of Japanese oak and other dense hardwoods. Resembling a miniature pyramid, this trihedral block had extremely sharp points. And like its predecessor, one of the spikes was always pointing upward when it was dropped to the ground.

Another wooden version was the *takebishi*, or sliced bamboo caltrops. There were many versions of this nuisance weapon, but they all still had the same basic characteristics. A section of bamboo stalk was cut so that a pointed, bladelike end was formed. The stalk was then trimmed so that the opposite end from the dagger point resembled a smaller knife blade. A double-ended pointed spike with different sizes and widths of wooden blades perhaps describes *takebishi* the best. Because of their near resemblance to a short 2- or 3-inch pin knife, they lacked the ability to stick upward under their own design.

Because of this, the ninja operatives used them in a different manner. Either the wider pointed blade or the thin, narrow one could be inserted into the ground along a path or other traveled road. Generally, dozens of these were planted so that the razor-sharp, tapered, double-edged points were protruding straight upward. Naturally, anyone who failed to see them and walked through a *takebishi* field instantly received a deep and potentially serious wound. This injury had even greater lethal ramifications when the unseen spikes were dipped in poison.

From these early *bishi* weapons evolved a wide range of multipointed *tetsubishi*, most of which did not require proper placement as did the *takebishi* variations. With the aid of basic smelting and forging equipment, raw ores, prefabricated links of old chain used in hardware, and other commonly disposed metal items could be rapidly converted into *tetsubishi* spiked *tonki* weaponry. More often than not, most of the *shinobi's* homemade *tonki* were created in this fashion or by a simplified hammer forging process in which the joining of metals occurred by pounding the heated component parts together. Later, crude sand casting was used to mass-produce the *tetsubishi*. After making an impression of an existing caltrop in the sand, the ninja could pour liquefied semihard metals into the mold; when it cooled and hardened, a copy of the one used to form the mold was produced. This ultimately sped up the manufacturing process and enabled the ninja to produce hundreds of these multipointed foot spikes in a relatively short time.

It also became apparent to the ninja that shape, design, spike length, amount of protrusions, overall size, and weight were important factors in determining the practical application of a given type of *tetsubishi*. The type of footwear or thickness of the soles worn by a potential enemy also weighed heavy in the balance of how effective the caltrop would be in the final analysis. For that reason, specialized types of *tetsubishi* were designed or modified to suit a particular mission.

Out of the situational possibilities evolved myriad new types of caltrops. These included ones with extremely sharp spikes over 1 1/2 inches long. Some veered from the traditional four-point design, having as many as eight thick tapered stingers. Given knowledge of whether the enemy was mounted on horseback, attired in armor and thick-soled footwear, comfortably dressed or undressed in private quarters while preparing for bed, or just suited for everyday affairs, the ninja selected one or more types of caltrop that would best suit his needs. This is where the *shinobi's* experience in weapon tactics paid off. Using the wrong instrument or weapon-tool at an inappropriate time could have possibly led to capture and slow torture.

Tactically speaking, many of the dirks, daggers, and shurikens found in a *ninpo* operative's *tonki* weapon pouch were interchangeable to an extent. A spiked *shuriken* could be substituted for a shiv, a multibladed *shuriken* could be gripped between the blades to create improvised brass knuckles, or the *tetsubishi*, depending on style and shape, could be readily converted to a throwing star that would stick virtually every time it was thrown. This was a common substitution tactic employed by these ingenious strategists when some of the *tonki* weapons had been expended during the course of a mission. The enemy could never know what to expect when a cornered *shinobi* reached into his bag of *tonki* tricks.

Tetsubishi that had more than four points were unique in several tactical ways. As with most caltrop styles of weapon, the greater number of spikes protruding from the core ensured that the weapon would stick to and penetrate the target. The angles of the pointed spikes extending from the epicenter were closer together; thus, when they penetrated a foot or exposed skin surface, several of the tips tended to enter at the same time and at such an angle that it could not be removed simply by pulling straight out. When a *tetsubishi* of this design was dipped into a poisonous concoction, the toxin would affect the victim irrevocably before it could be removed.

Knowledge of the ninja's deceptive ways and the possible lethal danger he could inject from such a seemingly insignificant nuisance weapon gave the enemy all the more reason to fear a caltrop. When several dozen of these weapons were dropped during the confusion of pursuit, where little time was spent carefully watching a path, a samurai warrior's carelessness could have catastrophic results. It was another shrewd tactic that the *shinobi* knew and used with great effectiveness.

In the shadows of darkness where light was minimal and paths and roads held uncertainty, the *tetsubishi*, when planted in advance or dropped behind during an escape, had other advantages. Whether the ninja was being pursued by warriors on horseback, a small squad of armed foot soldiers, or the like, it made very little difference. Once the enemy's feet or horse's

hoofs had been punctured by these unseen menaces, excruciating pain and confusion usually followed. Just the time that it
took to stop and remove the painful spikes was usually all that
was needed for the ninja to complete his vanishing act.

In instances where the *ninpo* warrior may have depleted his
stock of custom *tetsubishi* before fully completing his subversive mission, he could always rely on nature to help him out.
Even when dried water chestnuts were not available, he had
other options at his disposal. Of course, these alternatives
largely depended on the season; availability of animal, veg-
etable, or mineral resources; and naturally any implements
and weapon-tools remaining on his person.

Seasonally, the small kumquat citrus fruit and the ruta-
ceous thistles prevalent on these shrubs made excellent sub-
stitutes. By picking a supply of these round or oblong fruits
and inserting the pointed thistles throughout the pulp, a
makeshift *bishi* was created. Hundreds of these could be made
in a matter of 20 minutes or so.

The sharp penetrating bones of fish, small game, or the
like could also be inserted into other soft vegetables and
fruits. If clay was available and time permitted, the clever *shinobi* could opt to create unusual variations by inserting pointed slivers of bamboo or sturdy sharpened sticks into the
moistened soil mass. Once it dried, the points were firmly set
into the clay, thus providing him with a viable caltrop.

The ninja's many years of early training in improvised
weapon construction was a tool in its own right. With the creations that he invented in the field, especially any pointed or
bladed *tonki* weapon, he could extract the venom from toads,
spiders, and other poisonous insects and anoint the tips of
his *bishi* with it. This not only demonstrated his uncanny ability to survive under virtually all circumstances but his staunch
determination to carry out an assigned mission at any cost.

The *tetsubishi* and closely related *tonki* weapons were only a
small but very important part of the deceptive *ninpo* warrior's arsenal. Without them, many more ninja operatives would have been
captured, perhaps changing the course of Japan's torrent history.

Chapter Ten

CLEATED
WEAPONRY

Leather and steel, when cunningly synthesized by *ninjutsu* cult members, could be formed to create ingenious forms of armament and weapon-tools. Among the many diverse instruments of lethality were the *neko-te* (neko = cat; te = hand), the "cat claws" of the ninja. These were a set of ten fingertip weapons resembling the razor sharp unguals naturally endowed to cats.

The *neko-te* finger claws were made in many styles. Some had thin, tapered, spikelike protrusions stitched into finger-sized leather bands. The more craftily improvised types resembled a woman's long, sharpened fingernails. In addition to the leather and steel typically used to create the *neko-te*, natural articles such as slivers of shaved bamboo, pointed hardwood sticks, hammer-forged iron and semihardened metals, sections of flattened wire, women's hairpins, and even sand-cast varieties could be readily substituted and still provide the wearer with the same deadly results when used in close-range empty-hand combat.

Historically, it is uncertain which ninja clan actually invented these homemade unguals, but the many infamous ninja families that inhabited Japan during the feudal ages were directly responsible for contributing, at least in part, to the incredibly awesome arsenal of improvised weapons that

Iron and steel were common types of neko-te among the feudal-age kunoichi. Here, iron fingernails are fastened into leather bands.

were originally copied from animals, birds, and insects. It is known, however, that the *neko-te* was used almost exclusively by the *kunoichi* (female ninja) operatives. They were an integral part of the ninja clans, and their natural and pragmatic tendencies combined with feminine intuition tended to make them indispensable in covert operations, especially in making effective use of their feminine charms and being adeptly suited for using tools in the most inventive manner.

The *kunoichi* education stressed the use of smaller close-range weapons and devious ways in which traditional cosmetic or personal paraphernalia could be employed for the good of a mission. In addition to the *neko-te* cat claws, the *kunoichi* were extremely adept with such lightweight or less cumbersome weapon-tools as daggers, sight removers (*metsubushi*), drugs, strangulation tools, explosives, and throwing blades. Sexual enticement was often responsible for making use of such close-range weapons possible. The psychic and intuitive power of the female ninja operatives was also relied upon and considered just as valuable a weapon.

In emulating the actions of a cat when wielding 10 lethal *neko-te*, the *kunoichi* could unleash as much physical destruction as her feline preceptor. Like a cat who had been provoked, once she was close enough to her prey, the female ninja could inflict varying degrees of injury, depending on the situation. As with the instinctual survival traits of the animals, these were determined by the severity of the encroachment by the enemy.

A wild animal when cornered will only out of futility use

The cat claws of the ninja could turn an innocent-looking female operative into a wickedly effective adversary.

the necessary means to make good its escape. Likewise was the *neko-te*-wielding *kunoichi* who had been trapped or cornered. In cases like this, the female ninja operative may have opted to wound the antagonist just enough to convince him that his life was in jeopardy if her warnings went unheeded. Raking the eyes with the claws, ripping at the exposed opening in the frontal area of the neck, thrusting the five medal-clad rigid fingers into the face, slicing four deep incisions across the front of the forehead to induce a small but steady flow of blood to drip into his eyes, or a series of these attacks usually provided the necessary means to discourage the antagonist.

Should an enemy disregard these warnings and continue to pursue the object of his desires, the *kunoichi* would resort to more drastic measures. Once she was physically grasped or restrained, as with the animals of nature, she would take her

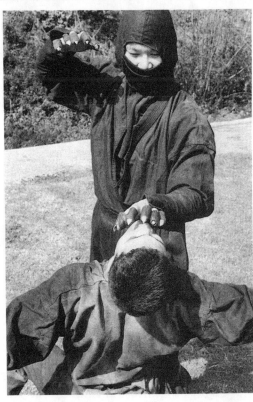

Several well-directed slashes and rips to the enemy's eyes, neck, and major arteries with the neko-te were usually all that was needed to subdue a samurai warrior

plan to the next more drastic plateau. These techniques included ripping into the inner arms and tearing at the veins and arteries. In a random and sudden manner, both sets of *neko-te* would rip at the wrist and hands of the enemy. The deep slashes to these extremities produced a lot of blood and excruciating pain in a few seconds. If the enemy's intentions could be anticipated, the female ninja could also use her basic *tai-jutsu* (unarmed combat) skills. Depending on the type of attack, she would use the appropriate block to deflect or redirect a powerful aggressive assault before swiftly countering with the 10 razor-sharp cat claws. Either way, the enemy was certain to get more than he bargained for.

Because of the woman's feminine nature and accepted status as a subjugated being during feudal age Japan, her

The element of surprise played a vital role in using the lethal ninja cat claws. An unexpected slash to the throat was usually all that the female ninja needed after she had used her charms to gain an enemy's trust.

fighting skills were often underestimated. This proved to be highly advantageous when the *neko-te* was unceremoniously extracted from the large open sleeves of a *kimono*. At times where a female ninja had gained the trust of an enemy interested in her sexual charms, this stealth tactic proved quite effective in bringing her suitor's life to a swift and bloody end.

In instances like this, the *kunoichi* who had earned the status of one of the household of an enemy camp or was called in to provide amorous activities for the enemy of a client may have opted to use the *neko-te* in conjunction with other instruments as a prelude to the finale. After ripping the eyes and blinding the enemy with the *neko-te*, she could then extract a dagger, long thin hair pin, or silk cord and take his life. Naturally, she made plans far in advance to ensure her escape before sentries or other household personnel became aware of his unfortunate and premature demise.

As with the cat, the *kunoichi* who wielded the *neko-te* was equally as treacherous as either the hunter or the hunted. Only her victim found out too late just how potent these claws could be!

Chapter Eleven

CLAWED WEAPONRY

During the course of martial evolution, animals have played a vital role in providing mankind with various and oftentimes unique methods of defending himself. Whereas every animal, bird, and insect has been endowed with natural weapons, humans have to rely upon their keen sense of logic, enormous mental capacities, and inherent superior intellect to survive in his given environment. Nature's creations have survived the millennia on nothing more than survival instinct and those weapons provided by nature.

Examples of natural weapons of the animal world include poisons found in the venoms of many snakes, fish, insects, and arachnids (spiders, etc.). Claws, talons, fangs, horns, antlers, and beaks have obvious survival purposes. Even ones not so fortunate have been adequately provided for in one way or another. Many of these lesser-endowed species rely on weapons such as camouflage, incredible speed, or highly attuned senses to forewarn them early enough to escape impending danger.

The ingenious ninja clans of feudal-age Japan borrowed many of the animal's natural weapons and survival techniques to expand their *shinobi* capabilities. For one that has made an in-depth study of the ninja's elusive life-style, art, and expansive weapon-tool arsenal, it is not difficult to see the many similarities with the survival methods of animals. The *henso-jutsu* (disguise and impersonation) arts, for example, were similar in many respects to the survival tactics used by the lesser-armed species. To change their looks, assume the appearance of something or someone else, or blend into the environment with such proficiency that they were undetectable were among the deceptive ruses shared by both.

Certain aspects of this synthesis were present in many of the weapon-tools employed by the ninja. One in particular

The shinobi-shuko were used by the ninja as both assassination weapons and tools for scaling seemingly impenetrable barriers.

was the highly evolved *shuko* (metal bands that slip over the hands, concealing four sharp spikes on the palm side) and *ashiko* (metal foot bands with protruding spikes).

Within the dark arsenal of the ninja, these simple yet sophisticated weapon tools were commonly known as "tiger claws." They were a set of fierce instruments that provided the ninja not only with a means of emulating the vast arsenal of fighting techniques used by the cunning and awesomely feared cat family, but with an enhanced method of using their *tai-jutsu* with a great deal more effectiveness, ultimately giving them the ability, in many respects, to exceed the capabilities of their feline predecessors!

The *shinobi-shuko* (assassin spiked hand bands) was one of the few weapon-tools employed by the ninja that helped proliferate his mystical reputation as a demon with eerie supernatural powers. Tales and legendary folklore documented incredible feats where these devils of darkness could fly, walk on water, live underwater like fish, become invisible at will, suddenly vanish into the ground, fade through stone walls, disappear in a puff of

smoke, and climb sheer walls like a dragon ascending into the clouds. Improbable as these tales may seem, there is a logical explanation for each. The *shuko* (and *ashiko*) was one of the several ways that these "phantoms" could accomplish such feats of delusion.

The Togakure ninja clan is credited with developing these cleated weapon-tools, which remained a secret within their family for several generations. But the *shuko* eventually became a part of the other ninja cooperatives

This pair of shuko contains four sharp metal spikes each fastened to leather palm gauntlets.

throughout feudal Japan. As with so many of the ninja inventions, as soon as their discovery became known, they were borrowed by rival factions that dealt exclusively in the business of stealth and espionage. This again reflected the *shinobis'* credo to use anything at their disposal to carry out their duties.

By design, the *shuko* took on many different styles and configurations, even though the basic functions remained relatively standard. The hand bands were typically made of one narrow and one wide metal band joined by a flat plate of a similar type of metal. Some were made of hammered brass, others of iron, and later versions were made of steel. The wide band fit in an elongated oval fashion around and over the fore knuckles and inner palm. The flat plate connector was bolted, riveted, or leather laced to the palm gauntlet and fastened in a similar manner to a narrow bracelet band that fit around the wrist. Sometimes these bracelet bands were open and adjustable to suit the user's needs, and other times they were permanently fused to the palm plate. On the inner surface of the palm gauntlet, spikes of various lengths and configurations were fused into the metal. Normally, four of these sharp claws were mounted, although some warriors preferred three or five.

The *ashiko* (spiked foot bands) were usually made of a similar type of metal, but they were entirely different in design. Because they were intended to be worn on the feet, only one large, flattened oval metal band was needed. It was generally open at the top so that they could slip over other footwear without too much discomfort. Cords of leather horsehide, sisal hemp rope, or fabric sash were laced through openings on the top side of the foot claws. Many times when split-toe (*tabi*) footwear was worn, additional thongs were wrapped around the *ashiko* through the space between the second and big toe. This not only secured the foot claws so they would not slip off of the foot but helped stabilize them so the cleats would not shift when climbing. Because of the extraction problems posed on objects where the cleats would dig into the surface when climbing, two other cords were normally wrapped around the ankle several times and attached to another loop around the arch and over the instep. This made removing the cleats from a soft surface such as wood very easy to do while keeping the *shuko* in place for the next step up.

As simple as the foot cleats may seem, they were very difficult to master. Walking, running, or climbing great distances put a lot of pressure on the ankles and arch of the foot, primarily because of the 1 1/2-inch or so spikes that dug directly in at the middle of the wearer's foot. The *shinobi* stealth agent had to get used to wearing such uncomfortable devices without compromising himself while moving silently, swiftly, and surefootedly.

Both the hand and foot claws were used in a well-orchestrated manner to accomplish feats such as scaling castle walls or other high vertical surfaces.

It usually took several years to acquire the necessary skills to use *ashiko* climbers in an appropriate and effective manner. It even took more extensive training to use them in combination with the hand claws, especially when the ninja had to climb solid rock barriers or sheer cliffs. Learning proper weight displacement, knowing when a cleat was solidly entrenched before putting weight on that foot, coordinating the timing for uncleating only after ample support had been acquired from two or more of the *shuko* and *ashiko*, synchronizing the pushing and pulling movements to prevent sudden slipping and falling, and overcoming the fear of heights when climbing with nothing more than these cleated hand and foot spikes were all essential elements in mastering the stealthy climbing crafts.

Militarily, the skills needed with the *shuko* and *ashiko* were even more demanding. Since these arts entailed mastering fighting techniques against weapons of usually greater lengths, the feudal-age ninja had to develop the necessary *seishin teki kyoyo* (spiritual refinement) to face greater armed opponents without veering from his avowed *shinobi* commitments. Since his engagements in combat were motivated by love and reverence for his inherited lot in life, rather than the mere thrill of violent excitement and danger, he had to be willing to use his weapon-tools, regardless of the odds, in any way that they conceivably could be used.

From the combative point of view, this was much more than an exercise in futility. It challenged the underlying principles of the ninja's whole existence, especially when one stops to consider using the *shuko* against such formidable adversaries as a skilled samurai warrior wielding a deadly blade of cold steel. These type of odds would be comparable to pitting a talented boxer wearing brass knuckles against a seasoned fencing expert.

So was the dilemma when the ninja embarked on a serious training regimen of learning to use the *shuko* for combat. This should not be confused with the many applications involving stealth and deception when using the tiger claws. In *ninjutsu*, this was an entirely different type of warfare.

As a superior form of brass knuckles, the *shuko*, because of its all-metal construction, could protect the ninja's hands when they attempted to grab a razor-sharp *katana* (sword), *yari* (spear), *naginata* (halberd) or the like used by their arch-rivals. In certain fortunate situations, the ninja could use the cleats to rip the enemy's weapon right out of his hand. This was a dangerous challenge, but when the operative was highly skilled in *tai-jutsu*, which he usually was by the time he had begun training with the *shuko* and *ashiko*, it was not as formidable as it appeared.

Using well-placed, powerfully executed ripping and slashing techniques to the enemy's eyes, throat, and veins produced instant excruciating results. Likewise when the sharp, pointed spikes were driven into the skull. Since the *tai-jutsu* arts trained the *shinobi* to use all parts of the body in combat, using the *shuko* of each hand made it possible for him to attack the enemy's weapon and a vulnerable target area simultaneously. Disarming the enemy while seeking mortal revenge at the same time was a favorite technique employed by the skillful *shuko* user.

The more exacting and refined methods of using the tiger claws could be found in the defensive blocking methods. These methods were generally viewed as last-resort tactics when complete evasion or offensive methodology could not be applied.

Using the flat inner-palm area of the metal plate, certain types of blocks could be made even against bladed weapons. When the adversary executed a lunge, shallow overhead cut, or linear slash, the *shuko* could be placed in the travel path of the weapon. This would temporarily intercept and absorb the weapon's force. The ninja wasted no time, after performing such a dangerous feat, in resuming his aggressive counterattacks.

Other defense measures involved combining *shuko* and *ashiko* techniques. While the *ninpo* warrior initiated fake attacks with the hands, he could kick the enemy with the *ashiko*. The recipient of such an attack would suffer almost instant excruciating pain in his abdomen, groin, or lower legs.

That momentary disruption was usually all that the agent needed to resume his attacks to the enemy's more vital areas.

There were many unique and clever stealth applications for the *shuko* and *ashiko*, which were perhaps the ninja operative's favorite ways to use them. Applying knowledge and tactical wisdom from any of the levels of training, such as *henso-jutsu* (disguise and impersonation), *shinobi-iri* (stealth and entering methods), *sui-ren* (water training), *bo-ryaku* (strategy),

The ninja shuko were also excellent weapons. Here, the cornered operative has been gripped in a restraining armlock.

cho-ho (espionage), and *inton-jutsu* (escape and concealment), and, in some instances, combining the *shuko* techniques with other ninja weapon arts were highly effective ways to silence an adversary.

Using the tiger claws to sneak behind an unsuspecting foe and viciously ripping his throat out with the piercing prongs, puncturing the spinal area at the base of the brain and instantly paralyzing him, slashing across the eyes and blinding him, smashing both *shuko* into the ears and puncturing the brain,

As soon as he's grabbed, the ninja rakes the cleats of the shuko across the antagonist's hand, forcing him to release his grasp.

The shinobi then attacks his enemy with the ferocity of a tiger.

117

and attaching a metal wire between both tiger claws to create a makeshift garrote were common ways of applying these combined arts. Since these claws of death were relatively small and concealed very easily in garments or a utility pouch, they were among the standard pieces of equipment and weapon-tools carried by a ninja operative when he had to travel great distances to carry out an assignment.

In addition to their military and stealth applications, the tiger claws could also be used for many utilitarian purposes. They could serve as a *kunai* (digging and leverage tool), *kiri* (borer), *tobi kunai* (for gaining access through barred gates), *shikoro* (saw), *kagi-nawa* (grappling hook) when a lengthy section of rope was attached, *chigi-riki* (mace) when a section of wood and chain was connected to the wrist bracelet, or as a *kasha* (pulley) when rope was weaved through openings in the wrist or palm gauntlets.

With some creative ingenuity, the *shuko* could be readily converted to makeshift utilitarian staff tools. By affixing wooden staffs with cord, leather, or wire, it was possible to create improvised hoes, scaling or entrenching tools, crude gaffing spears for fishing, and quasi-effective devices for sliding down ladder ropes, all of which broadened the versatility of this ingenious weapon-tool. It was a weapon definitely worthy of the moniker *shinobi-shuko*—the devastating tiger claw of the ninja!

Chapter Twelve

SYNTHESIZED WEAPONRY

The ninja's articulated blade weapon-tools are considered by many martial historians to be among the most ingenious and versatile close-range combat contrivances the world has ever seen. Whereas many of their foes specialized in martial weaponry specifically designed and used in a rigidly stylized and systematic manner, the *shinobi* shadow warriors exercised a greater amount of freedom in creating and developing highly sophisticated weapon systems from seemingly insignificant and common agricultural tools. Their vivid imaginations combined with a deep appreciation for weapon-tool improvisation and the uncanny ability to actually incorporate advanced combat fighting strategies made the ninja assassin one of the most feared adversaries in Japan's past. Their reputation was only surpassed by their incredible skills in using the weapon-tools in their arsenal.

The *kyoketsu-shoge* is just one of the bladed instruments that was invented by the ninja during these times. By design, the ninja *kyoketsu-shoge* was a potent weapon-tool that combined the qualities of both the short-handled *kama* (sickle) and the deadly double-edged dagger. Attached to this home-made dual-pointed double-bladed instrument was a lengthy section of sisal hemp cord or braided woman's hair. Affixed to the other end was a metal ring. Since the composition of such vicious looking makeshift weapon-tools was strictly the creation of the *shinobi*, they varied in many other respects as well. The blades may have simply consisted of a broken straight section of samurai sword forged onto a curved scythe blade onto which a homemade handle was fashioned using

The kyoketsu-shoge consisted of a short sickle and a double-edged dagger attached to a lengthy section of sisal hemp cord with a metal ring on the end.

two half-rounded sections of bamboo or other hand-carved hardwoods. These were attached with either bamboo dowel pins or tightly wound pieces of thin cord. In some instances the handle may have been borrowed from a sword whose blade had been ruined. Other more elaborate *kyoketsu-shoge* double-pointed knives were meticulously made by forging and pounding heated metals of iron or other semihardened steel alloys until a suitable shape was created. These versions were very rare since most ninja operatives always viewed weapons and weapon-tools as being expendable during the course of a mission and generally opted to create a weapon from existing materials.

The lengthy connecting cord that tied the handle to the ring was perhaps just as important as the blades themselves.

Whether it was made of braided strands of women's hair, tightly wound hemp fibers, thin sections of leather thong, or, in some cases, lengths of chain, the articulated connector had to be strong enough to perform a variety of utilitarian and combative functions.

From the pugilistic perspective, the cord had to be strong enough so when either the bladed end or the ring end was twirled, it did not snap or break loose from the connector. Likewise, it had to be durable enough to entwine the enemy's nonbladed weapons without being severed. In the cases where chains were used, these *kyoketsu-shoge* versions could withstand most of the cutting force of the deadly samurai sword, provided that a minimal amount of tautness was applied.

Also from the combative perspective, the connector had to be strong and yet resilient enough to be maneuvered or twirled in sometimes very intricate patterns. Since these could be used by a skillful *kyoketsu-shoge* expert to trap, entangle, confuse, or trip the adversary during an encounter, the cord had to be durable enough to prevent his victim from breaking it once he or his weapon had been snared. This was also true when the *shinobi* had to use his weapon-tool to tie up an enemy that he had craftily neutralized in an engagement where he had to temporarily prevent him from revealing the ninja's presence to other sentries or the like. Since the weapon-tool itself was always expendable, it was more important that it served its immediate weapon purpose rather than possess elaborate cosmetic beauty and ritualized significance, as did most of the regulation weapons of the samurai warriors. A strong, durable connecting cord provided the shadow warrior with practicality and nothing more.

Combatively, the metal ring attached to the opposite end of the handle was unique in several ways. It could be easily used as a gripping handle when the entire *kyoketsu-shoge* was twirled in broad arcing motions, and because of its inherent weight, it served as an ideal mace of sorts when that end of the weapon-tool was spun in the direction of an adversary. The bludgeonlike effects of being struck in the head with a ring possessing that much heft was enough to induce almost immediate unconsciousness.

Provided that the inner diameter of the flat metal ring was large enough, which most of them were, the bladed section could be inserted through it in times of need to form an improvised lasso. This instantly converted the *kyoketsu-shoge* into a garrote or hangman's noose. This was a commonly used *kyoketsu-shoge* tactic when sentry removal through strangulation or hanging was needed to silence an unfortunate guard who had fallen victim to a stealthy ninja carrying out a mission for his client.

Another unorthodox usage for the metal ring was that it provided the ninja operative with a means of gripping that end of the weapon-tool without actually having to physically retain it with his hand. The arm could be slipped through the ring and the weapon forced up snugly onto the thicker part of the arm. Then the free hand could be used in coordinated fashion with the other hand to maneuver, feed out, or manipulate the flexible connector. This naturally gave the wielder an advantage in fighting or using more complex techniques that would have otherwise required the use of three hands—an unlikely possibility to say the least.

Though considered a utilitarian function by most standards, the metal ring was also adeptly suited for similar armed applications. When the ring end of the weapon-tool was spun or twirled by a ninja in a precise fashion, he could wrap the cord around the enemy's neck or other extremity in a calculated manner. He had the options of restraining, strangling, or forcefully jerking his opponent off balance, plus the added advantage of the continued momentum of the free twirling weight finally striking a vital target area. Of course, these complex and highly advanced techniques required much practice before mastery was achieved.

From the purely utilitarian standpoint, this same methodology provided the ninja with a viable means of climbing. The ringed end could be tossed over protruding roof beams or tree limbs or for scaling other high barriers. With the proper twirling methodology, exact release time, and precise wrist-snap, the ring could be looped around an object. With a constant tension maintained on the connecting cord, then the *shinobi* could ascend the rope. This is another one of the reasons why the connector had to be strong enough without being too cumbersome.

By most weapon standards, the *kyoketsu-shoge* was relatively small and lightweight. This made it a favorite weapon-tool of the ninja operative who needed a multifunctional implement when traveling great distances. Some of these unique qualities included the way that it could be concealed easily within his garments; double as a rope when the ring and knife end was removed; provide him with a tool for cutting, chopping, and sawing; used to a limited degree as a grappling hook; serve well as a trench tool or digging implement; possess all of the combative characteristics of the *kusarigama*; and be used in many instances to pick simple locking devices. The bladed point of the dagger could be easily converted to a spear when the connector was used to attach the double-pointed dagger to a lengthy section of bamboo or other rounded staff. The connector could also be used for raising or lowering tools or equipment and, in some instances, creating homemade tripping devices when stretched across a path or roadway. In these instances, the cord had to be thin enough to remain unseen as a mounted adversary crossed its path. As the horse tripped, the ninja would take advantage of the situation and swiftly rush in and annihilate his disoriented victim, sometimes with the double-edged dagger that was affixed to the end of the cord.

Among some of the more sophisticated ways in which the *kyoketsu-shoge* could be employed was in the feed-out methodology. Artfully unfurling the connector as the bladed and/or ringed ends were set in motion provided the ninja with many devious alternatives to deal with an equally or superiorly armed opponent. The double-edged dagger plus the subtly hooked *kama* (sickle) blade was extremely lethal when it was snapped or popped like a bullwhip. By knowing the balance of the blade and the weight to feed-out ratio for a given momentum, and by predetermining the release time of one end (usually the bladed end) of the *kyoketsu-shoge*, the sly ninja could inflict a devastating wound before his antagonist ever knew what had happened.

The *kyoketsu-shoge* could also literally be thrown at the enemy without having to worry about losing the blade. If the ninja did miss his target, the knife could be retrieved by quickly jerking the cord back.

It took a tremendous amount of skill to wield the kyoketsu-shoge in combat.

Whether it be through throwing, feed-out, or singular expending methodology, all of which the enemy rarely anticipated until it was too late, the *kyoketsu-shoge* wielder had other tactical options at his disposal if they were needed. By skillfully manipulating either or both ends at the same time, two separate yet connected weapons could be put into play simultaneously. Against an enemy using only one weapon, this deceptive stratagem usually caused him to doubt his own fighting abilities, much like he was defending against two armed opponents wielding two different weapons.

Here, the shinobi quickly hooks his opponent's weapon with the sickle blade.

After successfully disarming his surprised opponent, the ninja swiftly moves in for the kill.

Naturally, the ninja *kyoketsu-shoge* expert had to be highly skilled to pull off such a ruse, but that was one of the traits possessed by these feudal age warriors.

Defensively, the *kyoketsu-shoge* lacked many of the tactical advantages of the *kusarigama*. However, the ninja was aware of this inherent shortcoming since he usually made his own weapon tools, and he knew all of the necessary alternatives to compensate for this disadvantage. These included techniques like intentionally avoiding direct engagements with sharp or bladed weapons, swiftly retracting an expended or twirling weapon when entwinement was anticipated, never committing to a defensive technique that would leave him vulnerable to counterattack or entrapment due to his own carelessness, and intentionally executing fake maneuvers that would require defensive follow-ups. He could also use another concealed weapon after intentionally entangling or entwining his *kyoketsu-shoge* in the enemy's weaponry.

Offensively, the ninja had to master many diverse techniques. To simplify the comprehension process, he was taught from a very young age that there were always several options (usually five based upon the ancient Tantric lore book of *mikkyo*) at his disposal. Though some had strictly defensive or evasive applications, the weapon's design usually dictated the type of combat stratagems that would ultimately apply to a situation. In the case of the *kyoketsu-shoge*, there were obviously more offensive possibilities than there were defensive or evasive ones.

After the ninja clan member was enlightened in this respect, offensive training with the weapon was begun in earnest. It started with learning to classify and organize the many techniques into groups that stressed certain types of manipulative methodology. Realizing that there were only so many types of basic categories of movement, directional attitudes, and the like, he then set about to differentiate between them and then seek perfection in the particulars of each form of movement.

This assimilation usually brought him to the conclusion

that all possible types of maneuvers fell into three distinct categories (especially so in learning how to use weaponry that had articulated joint connectors, as did the *kusarigama* and *kyoketsu-shoge*). The first was the looping attitudes. These included techniques like maneuvering the weapon so that entwinements, wrapping, and circling patterns could be performed after contact had been made with a particular part of the connector, ring, or blade. Regardless of whether the technique was used for utilitarian, defensive, or offensive applications, the weapon wizard obviously realized for the most part that the methodology was basically the same. Loops could be used to lasso a weapon or extremity, or simply to attach the *kyoketsu-shoge* to an object so that climbing could be initiated.

Next, the *shinobi* warrior developed an appreciation for the twirling capabilities of his flexible weapon. This realm of physical mastery included first and foremost realizing that the twirls provided him with a means of getting the *kyoketsu-shoge* from one position to another while preventing an adversary from knowing exactly what his intentions were. Twirls could develop enough momentum to make the impact with the weapon effective, keep one or more opponents at a safe distance until an actual offensive and/or defensive technique could be executed, or provide the inertia so feed-out techniques could be initiated.

Because loops and twirls were entirely different, each type of flexible weapon methodology had to be mastered thoroughly before they could be combined effectively. For that reason, the ninja *kyoketsu-shoge* wielder had to practice for years before every conceivable loop or twirling maneuver could be performed with flawless precision. Then he had to combine these two different forms of movement so that they could be used in either offensive and/or defensive situations.

Next came the meticulous task of learning how to catch the *kyoketsu-shoge* when any part of it was in motion. This could range from simply reaching out and grabbing the cord to the more sophisticated techniques of catching the spinning or twirling blade section. Learning to recover the ring, blade, or cord had its own sets of unique difficulties, but these functions had to be mastered if recovery was going to be used in the event that a certain technique accidentally missed its mark. Situationally, recovering the weapon was necessary if quick and surprising changes in tactics were going to be necessary in actual combat. If the opponent swiftly changed distances on the ninja, the *shinobi* had to be ready to adjust to a greater or lesser range to prevent his technique(s) from being interrupted. If the connected end of the bladed dagger-*kama* had been purposefully thrown at the enemy, quick jerk recovery was needed to regain control of the *kyoketsu-shoge*. This obviously included catching one or more parts of it to get it back in his possession.

Mastery of all three of these basic techniques usually culminated when the ninja could instantly apply his five elements (wind, earth, fire, water, and void strategic options) to the weapon itself. Naturally, the ultimate test was against an enemy armed with a seemingly superior weapon. For that reason, the ninja gained experience by practicing hundreds of twirls, loops, and catches against a training partner who intentionally tried to defeat him in a mock session of combat. It was the ninja's belief that in order to truly know the weapon, one had to know himself. In actual combat, one never had time to reevaluate his capabilities or rely on techniques that had never been used before. These mock trials by fire provided the *shinobi* with the insight into his own soul. It also brought him to the ultimate realization that the *kyoketsu-shoge* was something like a dagger, something like a *kama*, and then some. The enemy usually found out too late what the other some meant!

Chapter Thirteen
SWORD WEAPONRY

Prior to the introduction of firearms, the sword was one of the primary weapons used by both the samurai caste and the ninja clans. Though their weapons were similar in basic design, each of these feudal-age arch rivals viewed their blades of cold steel in very different ways.

As an example, the ninja stealth agents were not as concerned with the stylized *ryu* (formal schools of sword training) as were the samurai. The venerated vassals placed a greater emphasis on highly exacting and meticulous extraction (drawing) methods—so precise, in fact, that an entire art was created known as *iaido* (way of sword drawing). On the other hand, the wizards of darkness found such ritualized protocol to be of little value as it applied to their cunning craft of stealth. Perhaps the only tactical nuance that each had in common was refining a method of "quick draw" extraction. Even here, there were several disagreements as to the most effective way of getting the deadly blade from the *saya* (scabbard) before the adversary.

Since the samurai warrior acted with a proper decorum and with a deep respect for his weapon, his longer sword (*daito*) and short sword (*wakizashi*) were firmly secured under an *obi* or broad waist sash. Consequently, the extraction maneuver had to be performed with coordinated precision. A

The ninja sword was generally shorter than the famed samurai katana.

broad circular oblique motion was normally used to get his steel from its *saya*. This meant that thousands of extractions had to be performed before the technique was mastered.

The ninja stealth agents, seeking a split second more speed in their draw, viewed this quick-draw art in an entirely different light. By not restricting their craft to such confining circumstances and keeping the *saya* in a more accessible position, it was possible to use the free hand to control, maneuver, and manipulate the scabbard. He was free to simultaneously pull the scabbard away from the sword while the gripping hand pulled the hilt in the opposite direction. In

The ninja warrior was less concerned with traditional, formal methods of sword combat than his arch rival, the samurai.

The ninja were less orthodox in their approach to sword fighting than their samurai rivals, who relied upon regimented types of cuts, blocks, and slashes. Here, the deceptive shinobi takes a seemingly risky exposed posture.

The samurai executes a powerful overhead cut. The ninja steps back quickly and blocks the top side of the katana with his own sword.

this way the sword could be drawn almost twice as fast as by traditional means. (One of the credos used to express this method of quick drawing was, "When both adversaries are equally skilled in the art of sword fighting, it is the one that can draw and cut first that wins the engagement.")

In addition to this sound logical precept, the *ninpo* warriors added many other unorthodox forms of empty-hand and augmented weapon warfare to their craft that were not normally taught in the sword *ryus* of feudal Japan. Among these important aspects were techniques that included using the *saya* and sword together—one hand artfully wielding the sword and the other swinging, striking, or blocking with the scabbard. This virtually doubled the strategic possibilities while confusing and disorienting an unsuspecting adversary.

Also included in these tactics were methods of manipulating the sword while coordinating it with body movement. Since their swords were generally shorter than the famed samurai *katana*, closer, more controlled movements could be executed. This shortness, combined with lightness, also

The ninja counterattacks immediately with an unorthodox one-armed thrusting strike, a technique not taught in traditional ryu schools of ancient Japanese swordplay.

made swifter, omnidirectional movement possible. (Of course, this normally meant that more force had to be extended to generate the lethality of the samurai warrior's weapon.) Moreover, when the one-handed techniques were used, the other hand could be used for grabbing, restraining, positioning, punching, or climbing while the sword was still in action.

This was another distinct difference between the traditionally trained samurai and the *shinobigatana* warriors. A proud and noble samurai would rely predominately on his heritage sword skills when engaged in the *iaijutsu* (sword-drawing art) or *kenjutsu* (art of the sword) warfare. It was beneath their dignity to employ less refined methods of combat when the revered sword represented the soul and spirit of their being. Therefore, indignities like mixing various armed and *te* (hand) fighting arts were never put to the test in real combat.

The proud samurai warrior would never use his magnificent weapon for mundane weapon-tool purposes. Such a highly treasured and coveted blade was respected and treated as if it were an animate extension of its user. Therefore, many unorthodox weapon-tool and utilitarian purposes were not considered for such a masterpiece.

The samurai's arch rivals of lesser nobility were never permitted to possess such a weapon in the first place. Therefore, not being bound by birthright, a code of honor, or stylized military conducts, the *shinobi* viewed his simple sword as nothing more than a tool. It served his simplest needs with just as much importance as it did his sword fighting.

In many instances, the utilitarian and combative uses merged, especially when the operative was assigned to a distant mission where a minimum amount of equipment could be carried. The *shinobigatana* could be used as a "bush" knife to hack through heavy wooded terrain, as a pry bar for gaining access into locked doors and windows, as a makeshift spear (when attached to a pole) for gaffing fish or small game, as a form of hatchet, or simply as a digging implement. There were

A *ninja agent uses his sword as a pry bar to open a locked door in an enemy sanctuary.*

still other more exotic, unorthodox weapon-tool uses for the ninja sword. When the handguard was firmly attached to the scabbard using the *sageo* (scabbard cord), clever makeshift *kagi-nawa* (grappling hooks) were improvised. Hooking the square *tsuba* (handguard) through the forked prongs of overhead branches, the warrior could pull himself to higher elevations. Then, by replicating that process, he could reach astounding heights with nothing more than his *shinobigatana* and a lengthy section of rope. Along that same vein, lofty heights could be reached by using the *tsuba* as a foot pedestal. By placing the sword along the base of a wall or other barrier, he could step onto the handguard and spring himself upward the needed distance to grab or get a foothold at the next elevation. Of course, the attached *sageo* (usually connected to the sword and attached to the ninja's body) was retrieved so that his trusty weapon was not left behind.

Even the *saya* had some truly clever uses. Since it was usually made of wood and unadorned, the hollow scabbard could be used for storing blinding powders or other mixtures used in *ninjutsu*. It could be readily converted into an underwater breathing tube, enabling the stealth warrior to swim miles underwater without his presence being detected. The *saya* could also be used as an improvised blowgun. By using poison darts, for example, with ample filler so that the breath could be compressed before the dart exited the scabbard, a fairly effective weapon system was created, thus giving this weapon-tool more of a reputation as a sword of doom.

Another incredible stealth art was cleverly created when the *saya* and *shinobigata* were used in combination. One of the most common yet unexpected ways of employing this stratagem was to slide the scabbard out onto the end of the extended blade. In darkened environments within castles or enclosures where the ninja usually had to operate, the *saya*-sword tool served the purpose of a weapon with a built-in early warning system. By feeling along corridors, the extended *saya* could be used to probe the darkness. If an object or enemy was touched and it became necessary to engage him, a quick flick of the wrist and the blade was completely unsheathed. Then the *shinobi* was ready to inflict lethal damage on his startled adversary.

A variation of this sword fighting ruse was used when the

sword was brought into play while it was still sheathed. A swift, calculated flick of the wrist would send the *saya* flying in the direction of the enemy. While he was busy trying to block or evade the missile, the deceptive agent would cut him down with the drawn steel blade.

This lethal combination of stealth and steel coupled with the deceptive ruses of the infamous shadow warriors made the seemingly simple *shinobigata* indeed a true sword of doom, especially for the enemy who underestimated the skills and capabilities of these feudal-age assassins.

Chapter Fourteen

WEIGHTED CHAIN WEAPONRY

Many countries utilized flexible weapons in their military arsenals in the 1600s and 1700s. Even in ancient times, articulated armament served a limited purpose before weapons with greater range were developed. However, they reached their zenith during the feudal era.

Europe, Russia, India, and the northern Slavic nations applied many of the same offensive and defensive principles of articulated warfare that the inventive *shinobi* clans did with the *kusarifundo* (weighted chain). Most of the early flexible chain weapons were collectively known as "chain maces."

The chain mace family of weapons consisted primarily of a short heavy beater (end weight) of metal, stone, or wood connected to a hardwood or metal handle with chains of various lengths. Characteristic of many of the European maces were solid-iron spiked balls 3 inches or more in diameter attached to the chain. These were used primarily against opponents attired in full suits of massive metal armor.

On the continent of Asia, in Japan, and in many other Indonesian countries, flexible chain weapons were used extensively during ancient times, but their use peaked during the 1600s and 1700s. The Chinese employed various types of chain- and cord-connected flails against warriors mounted on horseback, as well as shorter versions where several sections

Three examples of kusarifundo weapons utilized by the feudal-age ninja (above, right and opposite page).

of weighted chains were attached to one handle.

Shorter, more manipulative flexible weapons evolved from this family of articulated weaponry. The one most similar to the *kusarifundo*, for which the ninja is credited with refining as a pure weapon-tool, was the Japanese *manrikikusari* (10,000 power chain). This weapon was a 2-foot section of chain with small hand-held sections of metal weight attached to each end. This style of weapon was devised by the famous feudal-age swordsman Masaki Toshimitsu Donnoshin. He named his weapon *manrikikusari* (man = 10,000; riki = power; kusari = chain) because he felt it possessed the power to disarm or subdue any opponent using any style of weapon, and that it had inherent offensive and defensive tactical qualities that, depending upon the user's imagination, could number in excess of 10,000 possibilities.

Because of his renowned expertise with this cleverly contrived weapon, Masaki Toshimitsu Donnoshin eventually earned a distinguished reputation teaching many feudal-era vassals at his *masaki-ryu* school. Later, other reputable *ryu* evolved because of the weighted chain weapon's combat effectiveness.

The amount of direct influence that the formalized *ryus* had on the ninja's development of their own particular types of weighted chain weapons is unknown, but because of the uncanny ways that they collected and assimilated fighting and weapon know-how (mostly by infiltrating formalized schools of traditional military combat taught to the samurai warrior caste), nothing of military significance escaped their keen sense for borrowing and adapting methodology that would make their particular clans' skills more effective. This included learning all that could be learned with a particular type of formalized weapon and then spending years perfecting alternate ways to apply it.

As with the traditional *manrikikusari*, the *kusarifundo* was ideally suited for offensive and defensive fighting techniques that involved dealing with one or more armed or unarmed opponents simultaneously. These combat techniques included hobbling the adversary, choking and full strangulation, immobilizing by entwining the opponent's extremities, restricting and encumbering a weapon, parrying and deflecting sword or other weapon assaults, ominously twirling the weighted chain to prevent one or more attackers from getting too close, and using the weapon in much the same way that a whip would be used. Of course, there were many instances when combining these traditional techniques were used to deter, defend against, or disable the enemy.

The ninja clans drew quite heavily upon the methodology

The kusarifundo could be swung aggressively to keep a sword-wielding enemy out of range.

The weighted chain could also be used as a stealth weapon. In this case it serves as an improvised garrote to subdue an unsuspecting sentry.

found within the *kusarigama* (chain and sickle) arts. With the exception of the razor-sharp scythe blade and perhaps variances in chain length, many of the same fighting techniques applied. In both cases, stratagems and practical uses were systematically taught to the novice *shinobi* operatives by a skilled *kusarifundo* expert.

This early training with the weapon usually began with the student learning the basic fighting theories behind its use. Within this realm of knowledge were the clear distinctions between offensive and defensive tactics, comparable ways that the weapon-tool could be applied to others of similar design, distinguishing between effective techniques and ones that were effective theoretically but did not work under actual circumstances, and knowing when and how to use the implement at the right time.

Next were taught the engagement attitudes, literally defined as the positions in which the hands and *kusarifundo* were held for executing certain types of offensive and defensive techniques. Contained in these lessons was learning which attitudes applied best when the enemy was using different types of weapons. This very essential part of training also included certain postures and various types of footwork that worked best against different types of weapons.

After the *kusarifundo* practitioner had successfully completed that phase of training, he or she was introduced to the two-handed attitudes. These were basic methods in which the weapon-tool was stretched taut with the weighted ends grasped firmly in each hand. The primary lessons learned here were using the tight chain for deflecting, blocking, stabilizing, and forcefully redirecting any opposing physical force against the chain, and learning to unfurl the chain while using two hands to perform follow-up counterstrikes. Simply by reversing that methodology, the *kusarifundo* could be used as an instant offensive weapon. Among the more advanced phases of this indoctrination was learning how to artfully and deceptively maneuver the taut chain from one fighting position to another. This created a base for inducing diversionary tactics to confuse the enemy.

Next came the more difficult types of offensive-defensive *kusarifundo* techniques using only one hand to manipulate the weapon-tool. The novice had to have fully mastered the two-hand techniques before these more complicated maneuvers were introduced. Included in this phase of training were methods in which the *kusarifundo* could be brought from a place of concealment (the *kusarifundo* could be crumpled or convoluted) and instantly put into action. Integral parts of this intense regimen of training included snap-strikes (like popping a whip); circular twirls for striking and deflecting; lasso techniques; figure-eight omnidirectional offensive-defensive techniques; entwining maneuvers against a moving target; proper feed-out judgment; instant recoiling methodology (in the event a strike or block missed its mark); catching the free end of the spinning chain before, during, or after a technique had been executed; and skillfully manipulating a single-hand technique back into a double-hand maneuver without faltering.

After this extensive training had been completed with perfection, the strike-to-attitude phase was initiated. This entailed the *kusarifundo* user learning and appreciating the special relationships between his weapon-tool positioning, body posture, and the offensive-defensive techniques he would choose to apply to a combat situation.

Since spinning, figure-eight twirls, large and small looping techniques, and close-range two-handed offensive and defensive tactics entered into this methodology, the ninja had to be constantly aware of his body position in relationship to his weapon. To not be capable of skillfully maneuvering in harmony with the weapon-tool extension would certainly hinder his ability to effectively defend against such an expert as the samurai warrior. An in-depth understanding of applied timing to a given fighting situation, agility, anticipated positioning and location of the weapon at a given time, balance, reflexive dexterity, coordinated hand/eye movement, distance and speed of the weapon, the opponent's rate of movement and weapon telemetry, and follow-up techniques were all crucial to mastering the strike-to-attitude phases of training. This orthodox phase was perhaps the most difficult to master since the *shinobi* had to incorporate all of the other previously learned one- and two-hand techniques as well.

Once this had been integrated into his fighting style, more specialized forms of study were undertaken. Among the first of these was developing strikes that could be executed with deadly accuracy. Knowing eight different strike angles per each one- or two-hand technique, what types of effects the strike would have on certain parts of the enemy's anatomy (throat, neck, temple, etc.), how much force was needed to achieve the desired effects, how to execute an accurate strike through an opponent's moving weapon and reach the intended vital target, and how to confuse the opponent with fake releases before an actual strike was executed were among the essential aspects of this phase. Though this was easier to learn than the previous regimen, it took much more time to master becoming consistently accurate with each type of strike.

Because each *kusarifundo* was usually different in weight, length, feel, and heft, learning to control the weapon-tool became a very important facet of training as well. A form of this control was introduced when the ninja began learning how to harness the force that occurred when the weapon was rebounding after it had struck (or missed) a target. If an articulated weapon such as the *kusarifundo* hits a very hard and bony target such as the skull, the weighted end may rebound back at the ninja dangerously fast. If it hit a soft, yielding target such as the trunk or torso, the weapon may stop dead on impact. Because of this crucial dilemma, each *kusarifundo* practitioner had to learn many ways to bring the weapon under control. This was made even more difficult when a different type of *kusarifundo* was used. Therefore, the *shinobi* placed a strong emphasis on the type or style of *kusarifundo* that he chose. When those were not available and improvised ones had to be constructed, he tried to make facsimiles of the ones he was accustomed to using.

After he was satisfied that he could handle an assortment of *kusarifundo*, the ninja then began another phase of specialized training, that of learning the many forms of coiling and recoiling techniques. Included in this regimen was mastering two-hand recoveries, limp-weapon recoveries, fanning combinations, whip coiling, and waist, forearm, and shoulder coiling and uncoiling.

Within the scope of orthodox techniques used by the elusive phantoms of darkness, there was the art of "quick kills." Though the term itself is self-explanatory, the technique was of the utmost importance. Even if an offensive or defensive technique was slowed down or missed the vital target by a bit, the maneuver itself usually still possessed the power to stun the enemy. This allowed for the delivery of a second strike, choke, etc., with no immediate serious opposition.

When the ninja operative opted to kill, he usually always combined two or three quick kill techniques, even when the first one may have seemed to do the job. The idea was to fully ensure that the enemy was really dead, because a dead man tells no tales, nor does he live to warn others of the agent's existence in the first place.

Three optimum target areas were used when quick kill was intended. The first two, located around the base of the skull, were slightly above and to either side of the central point where the occipital bone and the spine join. The skull in this region has a strong convex curve, so in order for the *kusarifundo* wielder to hit one or both of the fossae at the preferable 90-degree angle, he had to strike at an upward angle to the target area. The primary objective was to fracture the bone and drive it into the brain. Experience had taught the ninja field agents that if the exact junction of the spine and skull were struck with sufficient power, a dislocation would also occur, thus adding to the immobility or paralysis of the victim. Several field encounters also taught them that it was just as effective and sometimes easier to strike about three-quarters of an inch down from this point. The added objective could sever the spinal cord by dislocating the first or second cervical vertebrae. The *kusarifundo*, since it served such a useful purpose as a garrote, was ideally suited for this in addition to the many twirling and striking tactics that could be applied.

The *kusarifundo* had a very unique feature when the ninja considered the flexible characteristics of his weapon-tool. Since a powerful twirling or spinning strike could be made to wrap around the enemy's head, this vulnerable area could be attacked from the rear, even while the operative was positioned to his front or side.

The unorthodox methods that the ninja *kusarifundo* artist used in actual combat were what truly separated the *shinobi* from the style-conscious noble elite of the samurai caste. Within this category of fighting techniques were methods of simultaneously entwining the enemy's weapon and executing a devastating choke; performing multiple double-whip pop strikes in two directions; mixing his combined knowledge from areas of previous training in *tai-jutsu* (unarmed combat), *kusarigama* (chain and sickle arts), *kayaku-jutsu* (fire and explosive arts), and *henso-jutsu* (disguise and impersonation when the *kusarifundo* was used as a belt or the like); and fighting in the many ways that a lasso would be used.

The *kusarifundo* had virtually unlimited uses as a utilitarian tool as well. This multipurpose weapon-tool was ideally suited for any job that a short piece of cord or rope could be used for. Tying an enemy's hands or feet and suspending him from tree branches; securing parcels to one's belt while climbing; jamming interior or exterior locking mechanisms; bolting shut gates or entryways; as an unorthodox grappling hook when it was attached to the end of a lengthy rope and flipped around an accessible overhang; and even for setting traps were just some of the weapon's noncombative applications.

Because of the weapon-tool's innocent appearance, even the most skilled of feudal rivals were not totally sure of the many subtle ways in which the *kusarifundo* ninja weapon of illusion could be used—until they discovered firsthand in an actual engagement with the masters of deception.

Chapter Fifteen
THE NINJA SHURIKEN

Essentially, the art of *shuriken-jutsu* was divided into two distinct categories. One was based on the star-shaped designs and the other on the spike-shaped designs. Both could be devastatingly lethal when wielded by a skilled practitioner of the art.

Until recently, there were only 10 distinct star-shaped styles of *shuriken* favored by the ninja. The early designs included cross-shaped, four-pointed, six-pointed, eight-pointed, and ten-pointed configurations. Variations also included triangular, swastika-shaped, hexagonal, pentagonal, and three-pointed weapons.

The spike-shaped *shuriken* also were constructed in a variety of designs, depending upon the needs and skill of the shadow warrior. They could be pointed on one or both ends and range in lengths and shaft configurations from completely round to hexagonal, triangular, or rectangular.

The star-shaped *shuriken* were more versatile and required less overall skill in mastering the art of throwing them. Since the multifaceted points could be made to stick every time the weapon was thrown, the star-shaped designs were usually more abundant in the ninja's arsenal than the spike-shaped. The spike-shaped *shuriken*, if accuracy was expected, required a keen judgment of distance, velocity-to-spin ratio, rotation, and aerodynamic characteristics before it could be used successfully in actual combat.

The infamous ninja shuriken came in a variety of configurations. Each style had distinct characteristics that offered the thrower a wide range of techniques.

On the other hand, the star-shaped designs minimized the chances of missing simply because there were points on all sides of the weapon. This is not to say that the star-shaped *shuriken* was fail-safe. In fact, this weapon of stealth required a tremendous understanding on the part of the thrower if it was to be used as a lethal weapon rather than a simple nuisance or diversionary tactic.

The art of throwing star-shaped *shurikens* was an exacting science that required countless hours of training before the necessary skills were acquired. Details like *shuriken* composition, gripping methods, throwing positions, drawing, trajectory, penetration characteristics, sighting methods, accuracy, fighting tactics, knowledge of lethal target areas, rapid fire in the event that one missed its mark, moving targets, and multiple *shuriken* throwing techniques were all necessary if the *shinobi* was to use his weapon in the most effective manner. In turn, each of those considerations was essentially an exacting science itself. If there was a lack of proficiency, either on the part of the executioner or the weapon, dismal failure could ultimately be expected from the warrior.

148

A proper stance ensured maximum effect when throwing a shuriken. A near miss could have been fatal against an armed samurai warrior.

Equally important as the physical skills and a familiarity with *shuriken* characteristics were the positive emotional characteristics of the thrower. These included calmness, confidence, concentration, consistency, objectivity, patience under duress, deliberateness, perseverance, temperance to combative crisis, persistence, moderations in anxiety, and field experience.

The *ninjutsu* warrior was also keenly aware of the physical factors that had to be mastered in conjunction with these emotional elements. These factors included proper power for the shape or design of his *shuriken*; familiarity with the weapon; good hand-eye coordination; consistency in technique; proper methodology; good posture to ensure accuracy; proper gripping, body positioning, power-to-distance ratios, and release judgment; the right weapon for the specific task;

Although the ninja generally carried his sword on a mission, targets at long distances were engaged with the shuriken.

The ninja warrior could use one or several shurikens as improvised fistload weapons for close-in fighting.

and a full comprehension of the particular *shuriken's* capability. It is no wonder that the ninja was a master of his craft. The years of training prepared him for that single moment when he may be called upon to offer his skills and services to one in power. In the event of capture, these dedicated espionage agents would use concealed explosives to take their own lives and destroy their facial features so their personal and their clan's identities would not be divulged to the enemy. The *ninjutsu* warrior had to dedicate his life to his profession and be willing to die for the sake of completing a mission.

Chapter Sixteen
AIR-PROPELLED WEAPONRY

The ninja *fuki-ya* is was the potentially lethal ammunition forcefully blown from the *fukidake*. Together they formed a unique and oftentimes covert close-range method of silently eliminating an enemy.

In addition to their silent killing potential, the *fuki-ya* (darts) and *fukidake* (blowgun) could be used with great effectiveness to create confusion and uncertainty in an unsuspecting adversary, for spooking livestock or enemy horses, and even for signaling other ninja operatives when dire emergencies warranted such use. An example of the latter application was a secret message affixed to the *fuki-ya* and silently transmitted at limited distances of usually no more than 50 feet to another agent involved with an assignment.

The *fuki-ya* darts were not standard in either purpose or design. Even among the different ninja clans, there were no specified styles or identifying marks to indicate their origin and ultimately trace it to a certain clan member (as was the case with the arrows and darts constructed by many Western nations). Considering the nature of the ninja's profession, the inability to trace them added yet another dimension of mystery to them.

These improvised projectiles could be assembled from many materials at the clever ninja's disposal. Items such as

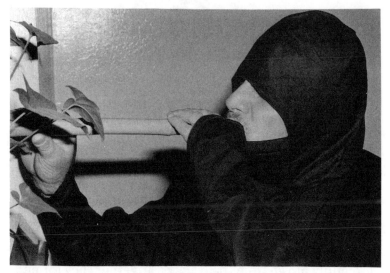

A ninja would lay in wait for hours until the time was right to unleash his deadly fuki-ya dart.

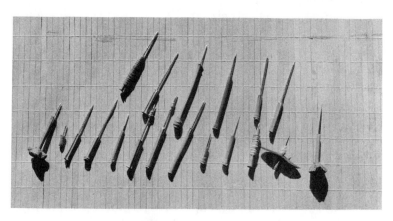

Specialty darts came in many sizes and shapes. Some were used for deep penetration and others for inflicting superficial flesh wounds. Notice the variations in needle length, shaft diameter, "fluff" diameter, and thread wrappings.

rice paper, slivers of metal, bamboo splinters, thistles from plants, tattoo needles, chopsticks, the teeth from wooden or metal combs used by women of that period, coins that had been heated and hammer-forged, any spiked *shuriken* (throwing projectile) that could be modified and honed to form a lightweight pointed tip, and quills and feathers were all used to make the darts. Dried bones from fish, animals, and certain horned insects could also be shaped to form the stingerlike points of these seemingly nonlethal darts.

When a sharp, slender missile was affixed to any number of lightweight fluff of fibers, tightly wrapped flaring paper cones, or berries that were of corresponding size to the hollow tubes used for the *fukidake*, this virtually silent weapon system was completed with very little difficulty. Unassembled, these common items defied suspicion by ones less knowledgeable in the art of silent warfare.

The ninja based the lethality of his *fuki-ya* on four different yet related elements: the length of the needlelike spike, depth of penetration, accuracy of the missile, and the amount of toxicity in the poison applied to the pointed tips. The relationship of these essential *fukidaki* qualities formed the basis from which many types of *fukiya* were created in the first place. Depending upon how the weapon would be used as a nuisance tool, spooking stratagem, signaling device, or lethal weapon, the four elements had to be mastered by the ninja operative before he felt competent enough to actually ply this skill during the course of a mission.

The length of the dart spikes was determined predominately by the inherent features of the item used for the point, but other factors had to be considered as well. These included weight of the entire dart, amount of lung pressure blown into the *fukidaki* before the dart left its pressurized container, actual shape of the needle point tip, composition of the tip in relation to the density of the intended target, angle of trajectory so as to minimize deflection, amount and type of poison used on the tip, how well the toxic concoctions adhered to the point, balance characteristics of each style of dart, and the tensile strength of the tip when it struck a target. Naturally, these elements and the many situations that the ninja could encounter affected what type and length of *fuki-ya* he used to achieve the penetration he desired.

To a degree, the length of the *fuki-ya* dart tip had a direct relationship to the depth of penetration. However, other little-known factors were just as important, such as the overall length of the *fukidake* (the longer the hollow tube, the more pressure buildup before the dart left the enclosure), drag resistance to lung pressure ratio (the amount of snugness between the fluff of fiber and the inside wall of the blowgun tube in proportion to the amount of blow pressure to the lip piece of the tube), the type of fluff fiber or conical flights used, the angle of trajectory, distance of the target from the mouth of the *fukidake*, amount of protection worn by the intended victim, sharpness of the point, and anatomical knowledge of the most sensitive parts of the body.

Though the depth of penetration had some direct bearing on the potential lethality of the weapon, the *shinobi* was well versed in the many ways that seemingly superficial injections could be used to kill his enemy. By knowing exactly where the arteries, veins, and blood vessels were located and how close they were to the skin surface, he could mortally wound an enemy when the victim thought that the dart was only being used to deter his threatening assaults. This was especially true when one of the many highly toxic poisons were smeared on the tip of the *fuki-ya*. In many cases, a flesh wound to the hand, exposed arm, or face could prove to be fatal when blood was tainted with these vile potions.

The accuracy of the missile was perhaps the most important aspect of using his *fuki-ya* and *fukidake* effectively. Without the ability to propel a dart accurately, penetration meant very little unless the weapon system was used as a diversionary ruse to trick an enemy into believing that his darts were indeed lethal. Usually the enemy discovered too late, in one respect or another, whether the dart was lethal or not. Of course, this was dependent upon his being struck with a dart in the first place.

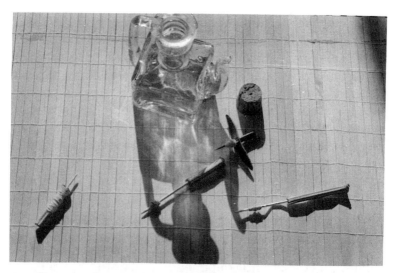

A small container of poison and a variety of select darts provided the shinobi assassin with a means of inflicting his own brand of silent death.

The flute could be converted into a lethal fukidake by removing the reed piece and covering the holes with the fingers.

As a vital element of every *ninjutsu* weapon or weapon-tool art, accuracy depended upon the shadow warrior spending years gaining mastery in his craft. With the *fukidake* and vast assortment of darts that he created, he had to know their inherent flight characteristics and the amount of lung power needed to get them from the mouth of the tube to the designated target. Elements such as distance-to-force (amount of pressure applied in relation to the distance the dart had to travel), how to gauge the elevation of the *fukidake* for long-range targets (short-range targets required less practice), and proper judgment of lead time (the amount of lead needed to triangulate and accurately strike a moving target) were among the more basic of these essential qualities.

He learned very early on that accuracy and the ability to achieve it consistently depended upon both physical and mental factors. These were known as the "human factors" and were considered as a harmonious balance of physical (ability to physically use his skills) and mental (emotional factors that affect physical actions) qualities. Then, since physical and emotional human qualities could be either negative or positive, he had to distinguish between the two and only concentrate on the positive attributes.

Among the required physical elements needed to master accuracy were factors such as proper power in propelling the dart, familiarity with the weapon system, good hand-eye coordination, consistency of technique, proper methodology, good posture for certain types of shots, proper gripping, proper positioning of himself and the *fukidake*, regular practice against stationary and moving targets, the right style of dart for the job, and the full range of the blowguns' capabilities.

The positive mental qualities, which lesser skilled individuals would often overlook, included learning to remain calm in life-or-death situations, maintaining a confident attitude toward the objective, concentrating, remaining patient, having and exercising deliberateness, staying reserved, exercising temperance, and drawing upon all of his experiences as they would apply to a given tactical or weaponry situation. Because

When a tubular section of hardwood or bamboo was hollowed out, it could be used very effectively as a fukidake. When the tube was not in use as a weapon, plugs of cork, wood, or beeswax could be inserted into each end to avoid detection and prevent foreign matter from blocking the tube.

these mentally demanding elements could influence the outcome of a combative engagement, the *shinobi* spent many years learning how to control and apply this wisdom to his physical skills so that he would be accurate when it was required.

The amount and type of poison used ultimately determined whether or not the *fuki-ya* would serve its purpose as a weapon of silent death. Since there were many types of poisons and vile toxic concoctions that could be prepared and stored until they were ready for use, the ninja had to know which ones worked best for the kinds of *fuki-ya* used. Taking into consideration the surface area of the dart stinger, the absorption characteristics of the type used (wood, metal, etc.), whether the tattoo principle of injection was used, and the amount and type of poison applied to the dart were all important considerations that had to be studied carefully.

The proper choice of poison was discovered by trial and error. The effects of different concoctions were documented after tests of nonlethal, semilethal, and lethal potions were made on animals. By knowing the effects that a certain type of mixture had on a pig or other mammal, the ninja could ascertain the effect that it would likely have on a human being of comparable weight mass. By carefully regulating the amount and providing a means by which the poison could be injected into the person (surface area or thread wrappings around a dart point, etc.), he got a fairly accurate idea of how lethal his poison was. This knowledge of ancient alchemy and its life-taking effects also gave the ninja operatives a true idea of the amount of time that each type, in a given volume, required to take effect on his victim.

When larger doses were needed that could not possibly be absorbed by thread fibers or be reduced to residue and adhered to the spike points, the wizards of lethality devised methods of containing the poisons within the dart itself, much in the same fashion of a modern-day hypodermic needle. The darts were constructed from hollow bamboo and dried thistles that had developed thin apertures through the middle of them. The liquid was poured into a small section of thin bamboo stalk and a hollow thistle with a snug, moisture-resistant fluff permanently affixed to the back end was inserted into the open end of the poison-filled bamboo shaft. When the dart was expelled, either by breath or pressure plunger, the thistle penetrated and simultaneously plunged backward upon contact with a target, forcing the poison through its hollow interior and into the enemy. As complicated as these feudal-age hypodermic needles may seem, they were relatively simple to construct, and any ninja could make one given a simple stalk of bamboo. When thistles could not be found, smaller sections of hollow bamboo could be used with equal effectiveness.

The feudal-age *ninpo* warriors were also cleverly creative with their *fukidake* blowgun inventions. A simple hollow tube of virtually any length, provided that a natural or homemade bore could be improvised, served ideally as a way to propel the dart. As a multipurpose weapon-tool, the *fukidake* could be used as a walking cane, underwater breathing tube, flute, or blowgun. Once the ninja operative embarked on a journey into the realm of silent warfare, he soon discovered that the blowgun itself was just as much a science as the *fuki-ya*. Among the principal technical elements of this simple hollow tube configuration were constructing it so that the desired trajectory could be achieved from the various types of darts; learning how to sight, aim, and expel air from different sizes of tube openings; converting a flute into an effective blowgun; hollowing bamboo so precisely that the bore was smooth and unobstructed; learning to modify a typical *fuki-dake* into a pressure plunger model; knowing the accuracy range for a given length of tube; and understanding the aerodynamic effects certain types of darts had when propelled from blowguns of various length-to-diameter ratios. In essence, each one of these technical elements took a long time to fully comprehend before the *shinobi* felt confident to effectively use the *fuki-ya/fukidake* weapon system. This task took almost as long to master as did his understanding of the vast arsenal of airborne darts.

Provided that the aforementioned knowledge had been assimilated, perhaps the most difficult technical skill to master was actually sighting, aiming, and expelling the dart itself. To the ninja this was much more than merely pointing his blowgun in the direction of an intended victim and expelling a breath of air to propel a dart. It meant knowing the inherent characteristics of a specific blowgun before ever attempting to shoot it. Then and only then did his primary concern turn to the tedious task of trying to consistently achieve bull's-eye accuracy.

The old adage "A gun is only as accurate as its sights" was applied with equal fervor when it came to learning how to hit a small target accurately and consistently at a great distance. To provide the means of accomplishing this awesome feat, the *shinobi* relied upon sighting gauges. Two incremented notched sticks of hardwood or stalks of dried bamboo formed the basis of this complicated aiming and sighting mechanism.

The typical aiming method most often assumed to be the

"real way" to sight-in a blowgun is to visually assimilate a target at a distance and then estimate the centered distance between both eyes with respect to the target. Once that has been determined, then the shooter would speculate as to the distance from the target and calculate the amount of drop that could be expected for a given distance and compensate for it by raising the elevation of the blowgun tube. In most instances, this antiquated method was only justified after much trial and error with a specific blowgun that the user had become familiar with. To the ninja, this form of sighting was considered very risky unless he was so close to the victim that it was impossible to miss.

The sighting gauge method used by the ninja was much more in tune with the precision applied to virtually every aspect of his clandestine craft—leaving nothing to chance, eliminating all the possibilities of error, and relying strictly on precision. The incremented notched sighting gauges provided him with the means of applying this same philosophy to the *fukidake* art.

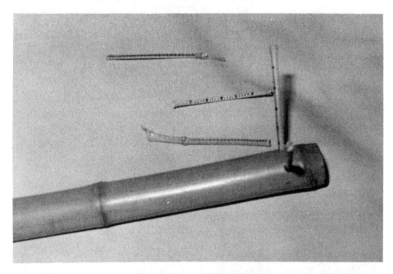

One of the little-known instruments that made the ninja such an expert with the blowgun was the sight gauge. These seemingly insignificant sections of notched bamboo, when affixed to the end of the fukidake at the proper angle, made it possible to shoot a fuki-ya with great accuracy for fairly long distances.

In mastering the sight gauge, the ninja first had to become intimately familiar with several important features of his own physical makeup: the width of the eyes from the center bridge of the nose, the distance from that point to the top of the upper lip (the point which coincides with the mouthpiece of the blowgun when positioned in the mouth), and the focal range at which the left eye's optic center crossed the right eye's optic center. (This was determined by closing one eye while focusing on an object and then shifting to the other eye and still remaining focused on the same object.) The distance in shift of the object provided him with the necessary information about his own depth of field to construct, assemble, and use his sighting gauges.

The notched sticks were affixed near the mouth (end where the dart is expelled) of the *fukidake* at an angle that corresponded to the width of his eyes (from the center of the iris). This assured that exact center lining (from left to right) could be established when alternating open and closed eye vision (left to right, right to left) was measured and compared to the width at the top of the notched sighting sticks. If there was a definite difference in distance between the object when viewed through the left eye than through the right eye, then the blowgun could be shifted on the lateral plane until the distance between the tops of the sticks were matched evenly.

Next, the notches were used to set the vertical elevation of the blowgun. Since the incremented indentations were the only reference points to gauge and compensate for the diminished distance from the center point of the nose bridge to the upper lip, the ninja had to deduct the measured increments from the known distance between his upper lip and the center point of the bridge. Once the technique was mastered, both the horizontal and vertical calculations could be performed very quickly and accuracy in trajectory could be ensured as long as the drop of the dart did not exceed the linear capability of the *fukedake*. Because darts varied in weight and blowguns were of different lengths, the *shinobi* had to rely upon his keen sense of recall when sight-aiming with a *fukidake* he was thoroughly familiar with.

After refinement of this secret sighting method had been mastered, the ninja was truly confident in his *fuki-ya* and *fuki-dake* skills. However, because of the many situations in which he may have been called upon to use this silent and deadly art, he trained constantly. Much of this regimen consisted of practice on mock targets that resembled enemies he might encounter in the course of a mission. He marked select vital targets on the mock enemies and put in hours of daily practice maintaining the skills that had taken years of dedication and serious study to master. The ninja knew that the way to total enlightenment was through his family clan art, and this art contained both life and death. The *fuki-ya* —*shinobi* weapon of silent death—contained the essence of both!

Chapter Seventeen

PYROTECHNIC WEAPONRY

Whether it be for sustaining warmth, cooking, frightening or repelling predators, providing light in the darkness of night, sending messages to distant tribal members, or for combat, fire has perhaps been responsible for more creations and inventions than any other natural element in the universe.

As with most civilizations, societies, or cultures, the ninja clans of feudal-age Japan were aware of the domestic and military advantages of such an awesome element and its many applications as a weapon-tool. Fire was so important, in fact, that more than 800 years ago, the Togakure *ryu* ninja clan saw its vast array of tactical and strategic advantages, and at the height of the historical ninja period (just prior to the unification of Japan in the early 1600s), had incorporated it into their 18 primary levels of training in the art of espionage and subversion. Many other ninja clans throughout Japan followed suit and began plying the art of their crafty trade while ingeniously using the elements of fire to benefit their anonymous clients.

Though no one nation, people, or culture had ever had a monopoly on the causes and effects of fire for either survival or military uses, the *ninjutsu* operatives of Japan's feudal past cleverly found ways to use it that extended far beyond the realms of known practicality during those times. Based upon their own unique viewpoint of perception and reality, plus the collected military wisdom passed forth from generation to generation, this knowledge tended to surpass the conventional martial pyrotechnology possessed by the other feudal-age military factions. Smoke, fire, and devious explosive devices were only one of the reasons why these *yamabushi* mountain mystics were so infamously irresolute and awesomely feared by their rivals. In an era where mysticism, religious beliefs, and supernatural abilities were attributed to spiritual enlightenment or demonic possession, the ninja simply applied their knowledge of the natural elements in ways that suited the purposes dictated by their clandestine way of life, leaving the illusion and mystery in the minds of those less knowledgeable in the way of *ninjutsu*.

This highly refined pyrotechnic art was known as *kayaku-jutsu* (fire and explosive arts), literally translated as the skills in proper placement, timing, and rigging of explosive, demolition, and smoke devices. The art encompassed fighting, distracting, destroying, eluding, misdirecting, and deceiving an enemy. In the later years, when black powder and other more sophisticated explosive formulae reached the shores of Japan, many of the older methods were supplemented by or replaced with firearms and their relatively unknown strategic applications.

Before the thirteenth century, before the Chinese introduced black powder, the ninja had devised many unique ways to use fire smoke and explosive incendiary devices from less sensitive combustible materials. These pyrotechnic inventions fell into six main categories: signal fires, torches, smoke bombs, flash bombs, sound bombs, and incendiary bombs. Within the realm of *kayaku-jutsu*, each of these specialized arts had numerous tactical and strategic applications.

Signal fires, whether large or small, could be either portable devices housing a continuously lit flame, or temporary fires set and extinguished as soon as a long-distance signal had been sent. Some of the portable signal fires were housed in metal or wooden containers with vented apertures that could be shaded or opened at will so that coded signals

The ninja used the pyrotechnic arts in many unique ways for stealth, deception, intimidation, communication, and combat.

could be transmitted at great distances without warning potential enemies of the sender's whereabouts. Others were simply set from existing burnable materials to transmit important data such as troop movements or the necessity to change plans or divert the enemy's attention while the real espionage operations were carried out by other factions of a ninja collective.

Among the most common lantern or flare devices were:

• *Noroshi zutsu.* An ash and sulfur mixture compacted into small balls and placed into a pipe. These were lit and used for signaling as the need arose.

• *Dobi.* A container for transporting lit kindling coals used for starting large, fixed signaling fires or setting off explosive charges during a sabotage operation.

• *Rosoku tate.* A multifunctional candlestick.

Among the most common uses were lighting explosive charges or firearms, sending signals when the hands were passed between the flame and the receiver, and lighting the way as a torch.

Torches, being one of the six categories, came in a wide assortment of sizes and shapes. Though they could be used as signaling devices, the ninja was more inclined to use them for other reasons when more effective signaling tools were available. In one sense, torches were defined as anything that could sustain a lighted flame under adverse weather conditions without being extinguished suddenly by a sudden burst of wind or precipitation. In this respect, torches had to be designed so they could withstand the harshest of inclimate weather conditions and be totally reliable when needed. Just any lit material would not do.

Some of these torches included:

• *Mizo-taimatsu.* Containing tree saps and hemp fibers. Because of the constant burning away of the outer layers, these torches could stay lit in rain, snow, or strong winds.

• *Tanagokoro-taimatsu.* A small hand torch concealed in the palm. These miniature devices were constructed so that the flame could be contained without emitting light that could be detected by someone nearby. When a minimal amount of light was needed during a mission, these torches were almost always used.

As weapon-tools, torches were used for much more than merely providing light for seeing. They were ideal weapons for starting fires, igniting explosive devices, and initiating smokescreens. So important was this specialized art that the ninja clans developed and refined sophisticated operational procedures for expediting these acts. Among the strategies were:

• *Hoka no jutsu.* The art of setting fires within an enemy fortress, bastion, or encampment to create confusion and chaos. These ploys could include, but were not limited to, setting fires to houses, burning stable quarters so that the horses would become frightened and stampede, igniting munitions dumps, and even burning granaries of rice and staples so that the enemy's food supplies were depleted. These were often combined with smokescreen ploys so that the ninja could carry out their clandestine operations without being seen.

- *Katagatae no jutsu*. Referred more specifically to torching the major wood framing of a building. Sometimes explosives or powder charges were incorporated in this strategy.
- *Katon jutsu*. A term used to encompass the many different types of torches, smokes, explosive devices, or combinations of these substances to facilitate an escape or avoid capture within enemy territory.

Several types of torchlike devices were used to start larger fires. Included were:

- *Oritami gando*. Tools that could be used as candles when folded in half. They could be extinguished easily by placing a hand over the mouth of the lighter.
- *Huichi dogu*. A tool that was used to light fuses on guns and other explosive devices. It was small, easily concealed, and was also used to ignite larger fires.

The third category of pyrotechnic devices was smoke bombs and related paraphernalia. Because so many flammable items could be procured, and so many dampening agents could be applied to achieve certain effects, the ninja operative had many smoke bomb tactics at his or her disposal. However, this refined art expanded to an even greater degree after the introduction of firearms (*tanegashima*) by the Portuguese in 1543.

Among the most common uses of smoke bombs were providing a means to enter or leave enemy territory undetected, escape capture when death was imminent, spook animals and livestock to create confusion, provide a means so that the enemy could not see his own comrades during a skirmish, disburse *metsubushi* (blinding irritants), and induce limited visibility in enclosed areas such as hallways, tunnels, etc., so that the enemy could not overtake the ninja during a chase throughout structures with which he may not be thoroughly familiar.

Some of the weapon-tool instruments that made these devious feats possible were:

- *Hyakurai ju*. A forerunner to modern dynamite. When this explosive mixture was combined with other burnable materials or *metsubushi* irritants and powders and compacted into a metal or bamboo tube, then sealed at both ends, makeshift pipe bombs were produced. When the fuses of these bombs were lit, depending upon the mixture, loud noises, massive amounts of smoke, and explosions occurred. The ninja had several hundred recipes for smoke bombs that could be used in this process, depending on what was needed for a specific mission.

• *Nage teppo*. Explosive miniature versions of the *hyakurai ju* devices. Sort of similar to primitive hand grenades. Depending on which smoke or explosive recipe was inserted, either or both explosion and vast amounts of smoke could be generated. Because of the smaller size, they could be expelled greater distances by arm power, sling shot, or arrow.

• *Dokuen-jutsu*. Variations of the *nage-teppo* hand grenades in which poisoned smoke was produced after the device exploded. These ingenious grenades were used with the ninja strategy commonly known as *iburi-dashi* or smoking out the enemy from a place of protection. Many of these smoke bombs became popular in the latter part of the thirteenth century after gunpowder was introduced to Japan by the Chinese.

Because of this new technology, where a violent explosion could be produced when heat or flame was applied, another category of weapon-tool was added to the ninja's already extensive arsenal. This specialized art dealt with flash bombs and associated devices that generated a lot of smoke and brief, bright flashes without necessarily producing a thundering explosion. When these loosely packed gunpowders were ignited or simply lit in their powdered states, smoke and flash were produced automatically. This characteristic enabled the ninja to create some fairly advanced effects that were much more difficult to produce with previously existing elements. As with the Chinese inventors, the ninja operatives were equally impressed with the bright and colorful billowing clouds of smoke and flash. However, the *shinobi* operatives immediately saw the tactical and strategic advantages moreso than their Chinese cousins.

Because of its newness to Japan, the ninja's first applications of black powder were used in a similar manner. Firecrackers formed the basis of this technology. Some of these ninja creations took the form of:

• *Torinoku*. Firecrackers generally shaped like eggs with attached fuses. The length of the fuse usually determined the amount of time that it took before the flash bomb went off. These mini flash bombs could be hurled into an enemy's campfire or down a chimney to cause immediate confusion. They were also commonly used with *hoka no jutsu* and *katagatae no jutsu* strategies.

In situations where several ninja operatives had to give the impression that many agents were involved in an operation, many of these devices were planted with a common fuse.

• *Onibi no jutsu*. The art of using fireworks, smoke, and other pyrotechnics combined with psychological warfare. *Onibi no jutsu* literally translated to mean "the art of demon's fire." The ninja agents used it to overcome superstitious adversaries by expelling flammable liquids and flashing powders from the mouth and nostrils of carved wooden demon masks. The enemy often would flee from the terrifying sight of one of these evil-looking masks while it was spewing smoke and fire.

The art of using *torinoko* expanded considerably as the *shinobi* clans became more acquainted with the propulsion and explosive principles governing their use. This wisdom and knowledge was usually learned through trial and error. From these experiments, newer and more sophisticated ways of propelling explosive charges came into being, such as using black powder as a charge to fire another charge that would detonate on impact. Hence, the invention of such ninja weapon-tools as:

• *Ohzutsu*. Reinforced wood and bamboo cannon. Metal projectiles or other primed explosives could be fired from this device. Many of the principles involved in the operation of this crudely built cannon copied the ones introduced by the Portuguese as they pertained to operating their matchlock pistols and rifles. The *ohzutsu* bazookalike guns came in different sizes and shapes, though the basic principles of operation remained the same.

• *Kakae ohzu.* A wooden pipe wrapped with fine layers of tightly compacted paper. These hand-held cannons fired small metal projectiles and flash bombs quite accurately for about 100 feet.

• *Tanju.* A portable propelling device not known for its accuracy. However, the sound of the explosion combined with the flash bomb explosives when the cannon fired was usually enough to startle horses and convince the enemy that potential danger lay ahead if he did not heed the noisy warning.

These newer applications of gunpowder eventually prompted the ninja clans to create and develop many varieties of makeshift sound bombs. It also prompted them to incorporate an entirely new form of tactics and strategies around the use of loud detonations to confuse and disorient the enemy. As with smoke and the effects it had on the visual senses, the noisy explosions had an effect on hearing and the nervous system. When both smoke and sound were combined, it seemed logical to the *shinobi* that the effects would be greater. But there were instances when only loud explosive sounds were needed to accomplish a particular mission. In these circumstances, weapon-tools such as the following were employed:

• *Bakuchi ire.* Thin casements of bamboo filled only with gunpowder and a small fuse. Though the smoke and explosive effects were minimal, the sound was deafening. These noise bombs were used in tunnels, corridors, enclosures, and the like to temporarily deafen and shock a pursuing adversary. The ninja agents wore ear plugs to prevent the explosive shock effects from harming their own hearing.

Bakuchi ire were also quite effective for distracting sentry guards when diversion was needed to break into a strongly fortified castle; forcing horses to throw their samurai mounts; planting false and misleading land mines to force an enemy to take another route; and planting real explosive charges to create the illusion that there were more live bombs than there actually were in a certain location.

• *Kayaki ire.* Any container filled with gunpowder. In addition to being the transporting container for the explosives, the unit itself could be used as a smoke or noise bomb when a fuse was attached. These improvised devices were normally only used as a last resort to ensure an escape when no other viable means existed.

The final of the six pyrotechnic categories consisted of the arts that were directly involved with incendiary bombs. These arts were more closely related to the explosive principles that pertained directly to the *tanagashima* firearms. Formulating ingredients to detonate bombs and armament, shells, and casings, and mixing certain stable substances to cause them to become unstable and susceptible to explode with very little impact was what this refined art was really all about.

This art was greatly expanded between the 1300s and early to mid 1600s. It was a time when the various ninja clans relied quite heavily on supplies of kegged black powder provided to the *shogunates* by the Portuguese and imported from China. For the ninja to gain access to this gunpowder, it was necessary to steal, extort, or exchange for sensitive military secrets of the enemies of clients they were working for. Yet since the supplies nor the availability could not always be assured to the ninja clans, the *shinobi* began to create and manufacture their own special varieties.

Upon acquiring knowledge through sources in China and the highly guarded munitions factories in Japan, ninja operatives trained in the art of *yagen* pharmacy began making their own homemade explosives. This, too, had its drawbacks, even though the clan pharmacist understood how to concoct such volatile potions. The basic ingredients consisted of equal portions of sulfur, charcoal, and saltpeter. The latter was the most difficult to acquire. Saltpeter, a form of potassium nitrate, was essential if really powerful powders were going to be made.

Surprisingly, as experimentation progressed, the *yagen-*

skilled ninja discovered this nitrate substance in its rawest form was more prevalent than they could imagine. Assimilating knowledge from the Chinese of how these explosive powders were composed, the *shinobi* soon discovered that they had an abundance of these natural resources right on their farms. The element of nitrogen—the natural ingredient from which the nitrates were to be extracted and mixed with the charcoal and readily available sulfur—was plentiful in the feces of livestock, pigs in particular.

By drying the excrement of livestock, which prior to this discovery had been used primarily for fertilizer, and carefully experimenting with blends of coal and sulfur, the *yagen* produced substantial amounts of explosive powders. Naturally, these formulae remained a well-kept secret among the ninja clans.

Through this same experimentation, the *yagen* also discovered that even the urine of animals, including their own, had a very important place in strengthening the charges of their homemade explosives. They produced their own unique blend of dynamite when ammonium, extracted from the urine, and potash were added in the proper proportions. Potash, being the substance from which potassium was extracted, when added sparingly, intensified the effects of the explosive concoction. Again, the right proportions had to be mixed cautiously if the stronger powders were to have the effects that were sought.

As a result of these clever manufacturing secrets, the ninja clans expanded the use of explosives in their subversive affairs. Using many of the older trajectory methods with newly acquired demolition techniques, they enhanced their infamous reputation to even greater proportions, making them the most feared enemies of the most powerful warlords in Japan.

The pyrotechnic arsenal of the shadow warriors continued to expand until they had virtually every type of explosive and propulsion system available during their day. Included among these mostly makeshift and deadly improvised systems and devices were waterproofed explosives for use under water, impact-detonating balls that could be attached to rope or chain weapons and spun into the enemy, land mines that blew the enemy sky high when he stepped on them, arrow tips that exploded on impact, and mortars.

When the knowledge and wisdom of *kayaku-jutsu* was carefully blended with the other ninja cloak and dagger strategies, it expanded their infamous reputation beyond their enemy's greatest fears—a fear worse than death itself!

Chapter Eighteen
FIREARM WEAPONRY

Hojutsu literally translates to "shooting art " (ho = shooting; jutsu = art or skill), but the ninja more commonly referred to it in reference to the knowledge of, use of, and exacting skills in mastering the firearm after it was introduced to Japan on the island of Tanegashima by the Portuguese in early 1543 A.D. Though the use of firearms had been known to the ninja since the early 1500s, it was not until they became available through trade with the merchants of the West that the *shinobi* clans procured them and began incorporating harquebus matchlock pistols and rifles into their already vast arsenal.

As early as the thirteenth century, the Japanese recognized and embraced the military advantages of explosives. The introduction of gunpowder and the many festive and ceremonial applications of detonating it with iron tubes, rocket propulsion devices, and fixed or hand-held wooden cannons used by the Chinese appealed to the clandestine clans almost immediately upon its arrival to the southern shores of Japan. This period of over 200 years had adequately prepared the ninja and Japanese feudal warlords alike in the use of explosive devices for military applications.

Among the first true *hojutsu* weapons devised by the ninja evolved between the thirteenth century and mid 1500s. These primitive *tetsuho* iron tubes were, in reality, no more than simple metal tubes resembling antiquated cannon, having only a small wick hole at the base of the breech and lacking both sights and a trigger mechanism. These cumbersome and ill-adapted contrivances were believed to be the first serious attempts by the ninja clans to develop a system of shooting.

As the function and practicality of these weapons became more refined, the ninja families' skills in subversive use of fire and explosives expanded as well. Both paralleled one another in technical advancements. In many cases, the skills acquired in one facet of this highly sophisticated field related directly to the knowledge assimilated in the other, thus making *hojutsu* and *kayaku-jutsu* fire and explosive arts even more important parts of their weapon arsenal. Not only had they become extremely proficient at placing, timing, and rigging explosive devices for demolition and distraction during the course of a mission, but they had, through trial and error, created ingenious ways to propel objects through the wooden and metal tubes in much the same fashion as the matchlock firearms that had yet to be introduced to Japan at the time.

After the real introduction of European harquebus (matchlock or wheel-lock mechanism) operated firearms, the name of these weapons became known as *tanegashima* after the island off of the southern tip of Japan where they were first introduced. The Japanese were soon making the *tanegashima* and within 20 years were applying the attention to detail that went into the exceptionally refined samurai swords worn by the retaining vassals in service to the mighty generals that ruled the various principalities.

After the major battle of 1557 (destruction of the Ouchi family by Mori Motonari) in which a general attired in full battle armor was killed by a long-range shot through the chest, the ninja clans of southern Japan were totally convinced that the art of *ho* was a science with even more validity than they had initially anticipated. Yet even though firearms were shown to be effective in combat when time for reloading and adequate preparation for firing were possible, the samurai warrior class never favored them because they lacked certain advantages in the heat of battle when thousands of foot soldiers were close by. It was their belief that a spear- or sword-wielding soldier could annihilate dozens of enemy before reloading or proper preparation could be made to get off a single shot from a gun. This disadvantage, coupled with the fact that the revered samurai sword was considered the soul of its owner's being, ultimately led to the decline in manufacture of firearms and stringent control of their use throughout Japan by 1879.

On the other hand, the ninja clans—since stealth, surprise, and diversion were vital parts of their secret societies—saw this as being advantageous in several ways. Adequate time and planning always went into a delicate mission, thus eliminating the need for rapid reloading methodology under most circumstances. Along with the restricted use of firearms by samurai armies, it diminished the chances, in the event they were discovered during an act of subversion, that they would be mortally wounded by a *tanegashima*. Hence, many of the ninja clans began refining and developing their own unique versions of the

The ninja realized the combat potential of firearms after a general attired in full armor was killed with one shot in battle in 1557.

Portuguese renditions. This was the "golden era" of *hojutsu* for the *shinobi* culture.

Confiscation, homemade manufacture, purchasing outlawed guns, and improvised assembly from different firearms were among the common ways that these pistols and rifles were acquired. Among these were rustic bronze pistols and small Portuguese derringers (*futokoro-teppo*). Simply known as *teppo* (iron rod), these could be concealed under clothing. They were wooden guns made from hollowed-out trunks of trees, the barrel of which was bored with iron or thick wrappings of copper wire, which strengthened the outside to prevent it from exploding when shot. *Kozutsu*, on the other hand, were manufactured firearms that usually had metal triggers and fired fragments of bronze, small chain links, and even iron balls. Although some lighter versions of the *kozutsu* could be held in a ninja operative's arms and fired like a bazooka, they were generally too primitive to be effective unless the *shinobi* agent was very close to his target.

To increase accuracy, several associated ninja societies devised one style of gun called a *hyakurai-ju*, a unique weapon consisting of several small guns set in a circle inside a larger reinforced wooden tube. Fired by an interconnected fuse, its limited rapid-fire characteristics increased the possibility of striking a target provided that he could maintain control when the volley was discharged. This was another reason why the skill of *hojutsu* was so important to the *ninjutsu* operative.

As the ninja clan's secret caches of firearms grew, so did advancements in firing mechanisms, propulsion, and trajectory technology. From the early Portuguese matchlocks, in which the primer (powder) was ignited by a slow match or fuse, many of their firing systems gradually began to shift toward the newly introduced wheel-lock styles. This gunlock igniting method, in which sparks were produced by the friction of a small steel wheel against a piece of iron pyrite stone, not only decreased the time for firing the gun but was more reliable in actually igniting the powder in the flashpan. In refining the art of shooting, this new invention proved to be a valuable asset to the shooter.

The shinobi warrior trained just as extensively with firearms as he did with the more traditional weapons in his vast arsenal.

Even then, however, there still existed one problem the ninja agent had to overcome. It was one of the same dilemmas that had caused the samurai warrior caste to acquire a grueling distaste for mechanized armament. This was learning to refrain from flinching or jerking before or at the time the weapon actually discharged its projectile. Historically, whether the ignition system was of the matchlock or wheellock styles, the weapons demanded a steady hand and calculated perseverance while taking a steady aim at a target as the fuse or powder burned down to the breech chamber where the main explosive was packed. As a result of the delayed-action response time, the shooter was never sure exactly when the charge would explode. This anticipation coupled with a sudden explosive recoil and thundering noise created an unnerving sensation. In some cases, the gun may have had a partially dampened charge, and it would go off later as its user was inspecting it, sometimes killing him in the process. To overcome these problems and still remain deadly accurate with one's firearm was a talent that very few acquired.

Once a ninja clan member had overcome the inconsistencies in powder-discharged weaponry and was experienced in his weapon's peculiarities, his *hojutsu* skills were just beginning. He began this learning process in earnest by learning how to correct a malfunction without losing objectivity or overreacting to an unexpected disruption. His many years of training in *seishin teki kyoyo* (spiritual refinement) helped account for his mastering this perplexing mental obstacle.

Next, proper care and maintenance of the weapon was extremely important. The ninja realized that any weapon, firearms included, needed proper attention and regular maintenance if it was to work when needed. With all other malfunction considerations to contend with during the course of an assassination attempt, a weapon that did not work right was the very last thing he needed.

This familiarity also put the *shinobi* shadow warrior in much closer spiritual contact with the weapon, which was also partially responsible for his achieving a stronger feel for the firearm. Becoming comfortable with it, letting it become an extension of himself, acquiring a confidence for handling it proficiently under any and all situations, knowing how to reload it in the dark, and being expertly capable of manipulating it without hesitation or uncertainty during times of crisis were all aspects of this firearm training. The ninja knew that the knowledge and feel of a weapon must be second nature during an assignment if he was to execute his instructions in the most proficient manner.

As with the technical and complex fire and explosive arts taught to the older and more mature ninja clan members, the next level of *hojutsu* training delved deeper into the physical attunement with the weapon. This was a period in which the clan member began adapting his *tai-jutsu* techniques to the actual use of his firearm. Instead of learning new methods of body positioning and footwork (which was the basic foundation of empty-hand combat), the ninja used familiar body postures while wielding, aiming, and shooting the weapon.

Because steadiness and comfortable and confident positioning of arms, legs, and body were extremely important and ultimately affected accuracy, this reacquaintance was necessary. Ultimately, though, the *hojutsu* artist strived to be able to shoot accurately from any position or posture, regardless of whether it was a standard *tai-jutsu* position or not. In most instances that required stability, stamina, shooting with deadly precision while moving, or the like, the basic empty-hand self-defense postures and stances accommodated this purpose quite thoroughly.

After the elder clan members were certain that the younger ninja had a strong grasp of the posture-to-accuracy association, a lengthy period of indoctrination into the deeper aspects of true accuracy began. All of the preliminary training in *hojutsu* only prepared them for this intense regimen.

It was the belief of the ninja that the mind, body, and spirit must be totally attuned if an objective of any magnitude was to be accomplished. "To think and to do are one and the same" perhaps best sums up the enlightened attitude of these mountain warrior sages. This assimilation of wisdom combined with trajectory methodology justified intense training in a similar manner to the regimen experienced when learning mastery with the *shuriken*.

Accurate shooting had a lot in common with throwing a bladed weapon. Among the similar mental-physical qualities were calmness, proper power, confidence, concentration, good hand-eye coordination, consistency in technique, objectivity, proper methodology in release, good posture, deliberateness, proper gripping methods, proper body positioning, appropriate power-to-distance ratios, and complete familiarity with the weapon and its capabilities. As with the years of training in mastering the *shuriken*, the ninja undertook the same regimen of practice until he was just as proficient with his firearm as he was with the throwing blades. Though this period was shortened considerably since the ninja had already acquired most of these abilities, he had to learn variations in applying these talents if he was going to use a single-shot weapon and ensure that his first projectile was going to count. In most instances, a *shinobi* agent never got the chance to fire more than one shot before his presence was discovered. If he failed in these crucial moments, it ultimately forced him to resort to other tactics and strategies to avoid being captured and tortured. For that reason, *hojutsu* became the predominate art of using and firing the feudal-age firearms of ancient Japan.

ABOUT THE
AUTHOR

American karate pioneer and promoter Sid Campbell
established his first school in Oakland, California, in 1967
and created the first karate program for deaf students in the
Oakland area. One of the organizers and original members of

the Northern California Karate Referee's Association, he has produced several tournaments, including the United Karate Championships in 1974. Among many other awards and accomplishments, he was named California's most outstanding Okinawan-style instructor in 1974 at the Golden Fist Awards and was named to *Who's Who in the Martial Arts* in 1975. Campbell is a prolific author and accomplished film actor, stuntman, and fight choreographer.